Jeremy Hardy Speaks to the Nation

Jeremy Hardy Speaks to the Nation

JEREMY HARDY

Methuen

by the same author
When Did You Last See Your Father?

Thanks to Geoffrey Strachan, Mary O'Donovan, Fred Sanjar, David Tyler, Debbie Isitt, Stephen Frost, Kit and Betty

First published in Great Britain in 1993
by Methuen London
an imprint of Reed Consumer Books Ltd
Michelin House, 81 Fulham Road, London SW3 6RB
and Auckland, Melbourne, Singapore and Toronto
First paperback edition 1994

All photographs copyright © 1993 by Fred Sanjar

A CIP catalogue record for this book
is available at the British Library
ISBN 0 413 69250 7

Printed in Great Britain by Clays Ltd, St Ives PLC

Contents

Preface

It has been many years since my first public speaking engagement. I happened upon my lifetime's work as a communicator of ideas quite by chance. At that time, I was working as an unemployed person. Today, that would be regarded as social security fraud, but in those days it was as well. A friend of mine who was a lecturer in politics asked me if I would speak to his students on the subject of graduate unemployment. In those days, when it was possible to receive a local authority grant in order to enter further education, thousands of well-qualified people joined the dole queues every year. Today, most students die of malnutrition long before their final examinations.

I thought long and hard about the advice I could offer undergraduates facing an uncertain future. I did not want to demoralise them, so I decided to take an optimistic look at the constructive and creative ways in which it is possible to use the extra time one has when out of work. When the day came, I overslept and couldn't get it together so I took some Benylin and went back to sleep.

I did not consider any further plans to make speeches until some months later when I woke up. It was a spirit of penitence which moved me to write my first real lecture, 'How To Pull Yourself up by your own Bootstraps and Make Something of Yourself'. My first audience were customers at the Kebab Machine opposite King's Cross station, where the manager had decided to give his establishment a bit of class by putting on readings, discussions, gallery openings and cider tastings.

I followed an interesting talk by a little-known writer called Howard Jacobson, who had traced the origins of smugness as far back as Clive James; and a reading by the Earl of Longford, the famous prison reformer and Christian intellectual, from his book *Alright Myra Hindley's a Child-Murderer, But at Least She's Not a Lesbian.*

The other two were canned off but I was spotted by a man booking acts for the All-England Folk Festival in Norwich. I told him I couldn't play music but he said, 'None of them can, that's why they talk all the time.' In Norwich, I was heard by a man from Radio Two who was producing a show called *Folk Folk* and who knew the bloke who booked the speakers for the Lord Haw-Haw Memorial Lecture, which was being broadcast live on Radio Guildford. Patrick Moore had had to cancel and they were stuck for a speaker. I rang the man and he said that if I cut the swearing, he'd give me fifteen pounds and a lift home.

This was really the beginning of my speaking career. Over the years that followed, many of my lectures have been broadcast on BBC radio, and from venues as diverse as the Festival of Mind, Body and Maudlin Introspection at Olympia and the Remembrance Day Thanksgiving Arms Fair in Canterbury Cathedral.

This book contains the actual texts of a selection of those lectures. Alas, there is not room in this slim volume for all the lectures I have given in my ten years as a public speaker. I hope that in the future I shall be able to publish a further volume to contain such subjects as *How To Stay Fat Without Dieting, How To Be True To Yourself but Lie To Everyone Else* and *How To Kill a Man With Your Bare Hands, and a Grenade.*

Until then, I hope that you will enjoy this selection. I think it was Dr Johnson who said, 'Oratory is not an art but a science. Science is the precise use of knowledge to postulate a theory, whereas art is more sort of paintings and that.'

1. How To Be Truly Free

1 How To Be Truly Free

This was one of my most popular lectures. I recall that it was particularly well received at Her Majesty's Prison Gartree in Leicestershire, where several Category A prisoners escaped while I was speaking.

In the course of this brief talk, I shall be focusing on the ways in which we can achieve that rarest of commodities, freedom. Of course, the only reason that I am able to discuss this issue at all is that, in our country, we have absolute freedom of expression up to a point. But even here in Britain, speaking to you today, there are things I can't say. I can't say I've ever read any of Melvin Bragg's books, for example. And there are legal restraints on my freedom of speech. For example, the police could prosecute me if I were to say something which is an incitement to racial hatred, although it's much more likely that they'd write it down and use it later. Moreover, anyone addressing a gathering of more than five persons is forbidden by law to call on the armed forces to mutiny, to demand an uprising against the Queen, to divulge an official secret, to commit blasphemy or to tell the hamster joke.[1]

It is doubtful whether anyone can have total freedom. When a man says he is free, does he really mean that he is wholly independent in thought and deed, or does he simply mean that he's not doing any-

[1]For more information about the state of our civil liberties in Britain, see my lecture How To Be An Adult, page 95.

thing at the moment? But even if complete freedom is an unattainable goal, there are things we can do to maximise the amount of freedom which we enjoy. These things fall into three categories.

1:   throwing off all forms of oppression;
2:   staying out of prison; and
3:   achieving inner freedom through breathing and relaxation.

Throwing Off All Forms of Oppression

In order to liberate ourselves from oppression, we first have to know that we are being oppressed. The great thing about Margaret Thatcher was that she left us in absolutely no doubt. But, as I intimated in my introduction, even after all our years of Conservatism, there are places far more oppressive than Britain. There are regimes in the world so vile and tyrannical that they make us look like a mere trading partner. Let us look for a moment at Iraq.

In 1991, the Western Allies went to war against Iraq, with the stated aim of freeing Kuwait. Because, of course, when we talk about being free, we mean free not only as an individual or a group but as a nation-state. Therefore, the Western Allies liberated Kuwait and handed it back to its rightful dictators.

In the years which have followed the war, many have asked why we supplied arms to Saddam Hussein, a man who was obviously an evil, bellicose tyrant. The answer is that, by and large, evil bellicose tyrants are our best customers: you don't shift much hi-tech weaponry to kindly old souls who haven't got a bad word to say about anyone. You have to know your market: starving Africans get the dodgy baby milk; psychopaths get the weapons. That is what we mean by Free Trade.

But what are the options for people living under oppression? Briefly, there are three: they can knuckle under, rebel or leave the country. Some people have fled the regimes in their own countries to come here. The British government does all it can to make asylum seekers feel at home – by treating them as badly as they were treated where they came from. The Home Office does, however, deport anyone whom it considers to be an *economic migrant*, along with anyone facing a death sentence or torture when they get back.

But what can we in Britain do to avoid being oppressed? The best way not to be oppressed yourself is not to belong to an oppressed group. It is frankly reckless to be female, gay or black in a society so clearly fraught with prejudice and discrimination. If you must belong to one of these groups, it's best to become rich and a Tory, like Joan Armatrading, who is female, gay and black. Curiously, the tabloids have for years told us that left wing councils give all their money to black lesbians. If that were true, you'd think Joan would have sufficient gratitude to vote Labour.

Of course, there isn't time for me to do justice to the whole range of oppressed groups in the world. So I've decided to talk mainly about gays, because not only are they oppressed absolutely everywhere, but all the other oppressed groups oppress them as well. Gays are also in a rather unique situation because you can, if you wish, hide the fact of being gay. Our society is quite tolerant of homosexuals who don't force their sexuality on others – by going outside or saying, 'I'm gay,' in a residential area. If you do your best to keep your sexuality a secret, you will be forgiven if you get caught. It will be said that you are basically a heterosexual who, owing to the pressure of work or over-exuberance in a crowded changing room, suffered a momentary loss of concentration and started having it off with someone of the same sex, and, so long as you didn't enjoy it, no harm's been done.

Prejudice against gay men has built up because of the HIV virus. Hysteria is rife. When I recently applied for some life insurance, I was asked if I'd ever had homosexual relations. I said that there was a cousin we used to wonder about but I couldn't swear to it.[1]

Aside from HIV, the justification given for the oppression of gays is that homosexuality is unnatural, although the people saying that are always dressed from head to toe in polyester. For myself, I am not greatly bothered whether a thing is natural or unnatural. After all, babies' incubators, dialysis machines, and Ventolin inhalers are unnatural. Conversely, earthquakes, wasps, stinging nettles, shit, piss, pain and death are all completely natural.

There is, however, a biblical basis for the oppression of gays. Leviticus, the Third Book of Moses, Chapter 18, verse 22, says that homosexuality is an 'abomination'. It is important, however, to see this in context, because Leviticus says all manner of inane shite. For example, Leviticus says that if a woman having a period sits on your sofa, you've got to burn it. It also says that if a man has sex with your donkey, you must put your donkey to death.[2]

Critics of homosexuality reject the idea that some people just turn out gay. Instead, they argue that people choose homosexuality just to be difficult; or that something must have gone wrong to make them that way; or that it's a temporary aberration caused by a

---

[1] Life insurance companies are naturally reluctant to insure the life of anyone who might possibly die at any time. They are at pains to point out that if you do die you may lose your no claims bonus.

[2] Presumably the donkey must have led him on in some way: by wearing a provocatively short saddle, or saying 'Ee-aw' when it meant 'Yes'.

lack of partners of the opposite sex, in a prison or a boarding school, for example. Here is a fly-on-the-wall recording made in the headmaster's office at a boys' public school:

Head   Come in, boy! Ah, it's young fForbes, isn't it?

Boy   Yes, sir.

Head   Two 'F's?

Boy   No thank you, sir.

Head   Now that's enough of that ribald talk. I've been hearing about your antics in the junior common room – your innuendo and overtly 'gay' behaviour.

Boy   Queer, sir.

Head   What?

Boy   I'd rather be known as 'queer', sir. Politically aware gays have now adopted an oppressive term in order to turn it round against our oppressors and also unite gays and lesbians under one banner.

Head   Poppycock! That is your nickname, isn't it, fForbes?

Boy   Yes, sir.

Head   Poppycock, there are no lesbians at this school, fForbes. There are no girls – a fact which is at the root of your problem: away from home, full of youthful vigour and burgeoning sensuality, surrounded by other boys.

Boy   That doesn't bother me, sir.

Head   It doesn't?

Boy   No, I'm a homosexual.

Head   You're not a homosexual. When I was your age, we all experimented playfully with the hearty rough and tumble of masculine camaraderie in showers and rugger

> scrums, but a man has responsibilities.
> He must put away childish things, marry,
> bring forth the next generation.
>
> **Boy**   Why do they call you Big Bertha, sir?

Who has the least freedom? The boy who acts freely but may be setting out into a perilous life of persecution, or the headmaster who endures the daily oppression of living his true life in secret?[1]

I have talked about the oppression of gays to illustrate just one of the reasons why the old saying 'it's a free country' isn't quite true. The reason that Britain has, since 1945, considered itself part of the 'Free World' is that it has a free market economy. One of the new freedoms which people in Eastern Europe are said to demand is consumer choice. Being able to buy the things that we want is at the heart of contemporary ideas about freedom. Under the Conservatives, many more people in Britain are now able to afford their own homes. You can pick up a sleeping-bag for around twelve quid. But what is seen as important is the *freedom*, the *right* to buy property. I have the freedom to own my home – at the present time, I'd just like to be able to sell the bastard, but that's not the point. At least people are free to buy it – they just don't.[2]

So, is Capitalism just a romantic dream that works in theory but not in practice? That depends on whether you're one of the success stories, the people who attain the level of freedom that only wealth can confer. Money

---

[1]During the course of my lectures I would throw this question open to audiences and received many interesting answers, ranging from, 'It is facile and glib to compare one person's oppression with another and only succeeds in trivialising both' to 'Are you a poof or what?'

[2]Readers will be relieved to know that I was eventually able to sell my flat, by dismantling it and selling the bricks individually.

is, as I suggested earlier, one of the best ways of throwing off oppression. You can literally *buy* freedom. You can buy power, you can buy time, you can buy sex, you can buy loyalty, you can buy industries, you can buy politicians, you can buy my flat but you bloody won't. Money can buy you just about anything except love or a pair of jeans without a silly label on the back pocket.

And, of course, the rich seldom end up in jail. If they do, it's an open prison, as happened in the Guinness case. The Guinness people were really only scapegoats for what is standard business practice. They probably only got arrested because Guinness comes from Ireland. Their stretches were relatively cushy, but, no matter how relaxed the regime, being in any prison is about as unfree as you can get. Therefore, in the next part of my lecture I shall endeavour to show you how not to get there.[1]

Staying Out of Prison

It has become increasingly apparent that, as far as keeping out of prison is concerned, being innocent doesn't necessarily help. Once you're in, the government hates to let you go. But there are so many miscarriages of justice waiting to come to court that ministers are considering proposals to allow the innocent to open their own self-managing trust prisons and release themselves.

It is very embarrassing for the system of justice to be shown to have failed someone. Such a situation puts the system itself on trial, although, since the system conducts the trial itself, it usually finds itself not guilty.

---

[1]Obviously, for those inmates of Gartree who weren't able to use the distraction of my lecture to stage a break-out, my advice was too late to be of much use.

Fortunately, the police don't make mistakes very often. They usually fit people up deliberately. Much of the problem of wrongful convictions has arisen because of the sheer numbers of people who are Irish: so do try to avoid this if you can. Remember that under the Prevention of Terrorism Act, you can be held for seven days without being charged – or, indeed, seventeen years without being guilty.

There is a man in Parkhurst Prison called Danny McNamee, who is doing twenty-five years for conspiracy to cause explosions. He is innocent, something which is nowadays regarded as a legal technicality. The evidence against him is forensic. Despite police protestations to the contrary, the forensic tests on Judith Ward, the Maguires and the Birmingham Six proved only that the suspects' hands had come into contact with police forensic scientists. But the courts in England and Wales still believe that a *fingerprint* is conclusive evidence.

What appear to be Danny McNamee's fingerprints are on bits of masking tape said to be from arms caches. Danny didn't make the bombs, so how might the fingerprints have got there? Well, surprisingly, it's actually quite easy to move someone's fingerprints from something they have touched to something they haven't touched. All you need is some ordinary sticky tape. And I'm going to show you how to do it.[1] You will need:

A plastic coffee cup
Some ordinary sticky tape
An inkpad
Some paper

---

[1] I originally devised this practical demonstration when I was asked to deliver this lecture to police cadets at Hendon. It went so well that I kept it in. The reader must visualise the materials to which I refer in the text.

Here's what you do:

1: To get prints on cup, fill with coffee and give to person under interrogation.
2: Remove cup. Cut small piece of sticky tape and place carefully on cup, covering fingerprint.
3: Peel tape off. Print is now on sticky tape.
4: Use print to decorate piece of evidence, e.g. U-Boat torpedo from Second World War. Place tape on evidence and press firmly so charges stick.
5: Get suspect to use inkpad to do finger painting on sheet of paper.
6: Compare this picture with prints on bomb. You will see you have made a perfect frame.
7: Charge suspect.

If you are a suspect and you come to trial in Northern Ireland, you can expect to face a court with no jury. But even a jury is no guarantee of a fair trial, as I found out when I did jury service myself, as part of the research for this lecture. Some of you will know the wonderful Sidney Lumet film, *Twelve Angry Men*, starring Henry Fonda. That film was very like my experience except that on a real jury, everyone is like the Ed Begley character.[1] What I mean by this is that the process of selection for jury service is a totally random and fair one whereby an entirely abstract list is drawn up to provide a random sample from a representative cross-section of lower-middle-class suburban bigots. And I found myself sitting with these people in a small room deciding the vital matter of another man's freedom. Here is a recording I made secretly:

[1]At this point the film buffs in the audience would nod sagely, not having the slightest idea what I was talking about, then run off home afterwards and look it up in *Halliwell's Film Guide*.

Man (1)	My mind's made up.
Woman (1)	Yes, it's open and shut in my opinion.
Man (2)	It's just so irritating them making us sit around like this when he's so obviously guilty.
JH	Don't you think we should wait until we hear what he's been charged with before we make our minds up?
Man (3)	No! I mean, look at him.
Woman (2)	It's written all over him.
Man (4)	Yes, you can see from the look on his face he's no stranger to this sort of situation. I bet he's been here dozens of times.
JH	I expect he has. That was the judge you were looking at.

This provides an insight into why we don't have black judges in Britain; most juries would convict them. Again, for a defendant, try to be white if you can.

Anyway, once the trial kicks off, you will have to sit through unending crap while people with bath mats on their heads speak Latin. Your trial could last for weeks and months and be very confusing so you'll just have to hope the jury are paying attention. If they are confused, they can ask the judge questions by handing a note to the clerk of the court. My question to the judge was: 'Don't you think you're getting a bit old for this sort of thing?'

In general, if you're in the dock, your whole future depends on the jury, and you will need, as in *Twelve Angry Men*, a voice of sanity and reason among them.[1] You will depend on the jury believing you instead of the prosecution and the police. If there's no real case

[1] I have to say that I was a splendid juror. I played the Henry Fonda role perfectly. Unfortunately, I played the Henry Fonda role from *On Golden Pond*. It was accurate, but it didn't help much.

against you, the Crown will have to rely on you being black, Irish, shifty or having a strong regional accent to secure a conviction.[1] But to help sway the jury they will use what's called 'Circumstantial Evidence', which means any old bollocks they can dredge up; your O-Level results, star sign, and so forth.

Of course, the burden of proof is on the prosecution. You don't have to prove anything – you don't even have to testify if you don't want to. All you have to do is to demonstrate to the court that you are untainted by all worldly things and that you were dead at the time the offence took place. And you'll just have to hope that you get a fair summing up from the judge. This is unlikely. Here is a model summing up from a first-year training manual for judges.

> Members of the jury. You have heard that the accused was carrying a sum of cash at the time of his arrest. You may think that thirty-five pounds is a very large sum to be in a man's pocket. You may indeed ask, 'If he's not a drug dealer why doesn't he keep it in the building society? Think of the interest he's losing.' That is a matter for you. You have heard that, when arrested, he failed to produce his driving licence. In his defence, his counsel has told you that the defendant does not have a car. You may make of that what you will. You have heard also from Police Constable Lane, who I hope will not be embarrassed when I compliment him on the clarity and convincing nature of his testimony, his firm honest jaw and a complexion to die for. Constable Lane has testified that the accused refused to answer questions when first arrested. But, members of the jury, a suspect exercising his right to silence is not necessarily to be construed as evidence of guilt, even though, in this

---

[1]In retrospect, this was a trite remark. The British legal system has a number of safeguards to ensure that more or less anybody can be stitched up.

instance, it is. As to the manner of the arrest, Counsel for the Defence has said that excessive force was used to apprehend the suspect. But, members of the jury, is it excessive to use four helicopter gunships to subdue a man asleep in a deckchair? In closing, allow me to make one last puddle. Thank you.

If you do end up in prison, you have, in a real sense, lost your freedom. But let us look at inner freedom.

Achieving Inner Freedom Through Breathing and Relaxation

The human spirit has survived any amount of oppression. Many people walking around at liberty have thinking which is far more restricted and distorted than that of people behind bars. The great Russian anarchist Bakunin did much of his best thinking in jail, although, of course, there wasn't much point in him thinking, 'I think I'll nip out for a bit.'

In this context, being free is not about our physical situation, it is a mental attitude. In this stressful, aggressive period of history, many people look to unconventional philosophies to give them inner peace. A friend of mine stays for days floating blindfold in a bath of lukewarm hazelnut oil, with the amplified calls of dolphins playing backwards on her Walkman, while a druid priest sings 'Those Lazy, Hazy, Crazy Days of Summer' from on top of the bathroom cabinet. I asked her why she does this and she said, 'It helps keep me sane.'

The rituals of new-age fads are no more bizarre than the rituals of established religions. It's just a question of what you're used to. It's very easy to sneer at things you don't understand, and I don't understand why more people don't sneer at them. But if something brings you peace and happiness, does anyone else have the right to mock it, whether it's yoga, Christianity, Chocolate Hobnobs or heroin? All have been said to free the mind, apart from Chocolate Hobnobs. Do they free it, or do they, in relaxing it, also pacify it, numb it and enslave it? Marx said that religion is the opium of the people, although the Church of England is more the paracetamol. And Catholicism and Judaism are the speed: because just when you think you're over them, they catch up with you again. Buddhism must be the alcohol because it makes you say really stupid things over and over and over again.

In many ways, religion does the opposite of freeing us, it circumscribes us – especially Judaism. Religious books are full of lists of things we're not allowed to do, many of which are highly enjoyable. But perhaps by abstention we free ourselves from the fetishism of sensual gratification and experience a higher non-secular sense of pleasure. It doesn't sound very likely though, does it?

If you wish to experience true inner freedom, let your mind imagine the unimaginable, let your intellect believe the unbelievable and let your senses explore the darkest avenues of your soul. But no dirty stuff obviously, because that would be wrong.

Of course, thought does not exist in a vacuum. How we think is a product of environment, education, culture, and how pissed we are. But inner freedom is not just about thought. It can depend on your being physically relaxed. You can relax by doing breathing exercises, which are very easy exercises to do because most of them involve lying on the floor, and breathing which is a piece of cake because you're probably doing that anyway. Alternatively, many Eastern forms of exercise can teach you muscle toning, physical and mental relaxation, spiritual enlightenment and how to kick the shit out of people all at the same time.

You might see Chinese people doing Tai Chi exercises in the park. If you wonder why they do it in the open air the reasons are cultural and philosophical. If you see white people doing Tai Chi in the open air, it's because they're arseholes who like showing off.

Ultimately, to achieve inner freedom, only you can decide what's right for you. But how do our three routes to freedom compare, in terms of cost, comfort and refreshment facilities? All are time-consuming and demanding in today's busy lifestyle. So, our choice of method for achieving freedom will be dictated by what we perceive freedom to be. As we have seen, freedom is a complex and subtle concept; and freedom means different things to different people. For a political prisoner in a dictatorship, freedom means the right to follow your own conscience, yet for an advertising executive, freedom means a ready frozen tampon you can pop in the dishwasher.

Questions and Answers

I always faced a barrage of questions after delivering this lecture. Here are some of them:

A lady in Yeovil Maltings asked me, 'Mr Hardy, I have a teenage daughter who is, well, rather wild. Do you think I'm allowing her too much freedom?'

I replied, 'Your daughter must learn that with freedom comes responsibility. So make a deal with her. Tell her that she can go to all-night raves, get E-ed out of her box and have sex with weird boys in the car park, but she also has to help out around the home.'

A prisoner at Gartree asked me, 'How can a man have spiritual peace when his freedom has been taken away from him because of a crime he did not commit?'

I answered thus, 'There is an inspiring protest song by Bob Dylan called "I Shall Be Released", which has given encouragement to many prisoners over the years. But a better one is "Up on the Roof" by the Drifters.'

Several people in different towns asked me, 'Does private enterprise guarantee freedom or slavery?'
My answer was usually this, 'A free market economy gives every worker a choice. If they do not like their conditions of work, their pay or the way they are treated, they can always mutter under their breath.'

A student in Southampton asked, 'When you speak of freedom as a state of being, don't you really mean the enjoyment of various *individual* freedoms to do *specific* things?'
My answer was, 'Yes, so?'

2. How To Stay Alive for as Long as You Possibly Can

2 How To Stay Alive for as Long as You Possibly Can

It is perhaps an indication of the human desire for immortality that this was by far the best-attended of my lectures. Wherever I went, I found that there was enormous interest in the subject of staying alive. In fact, when tickets went on sale at the National Exhibition Centre in Birmingham, several people were killed in the rush.

To assist those of you who wish to take notes, I have divided my thesis into three parts.
  1: Looking good and feeling fit;
  2: Stopping other people from killing you; and
  3: Clinging on to the will to live.

Looking Good and Feeling Fit

You might think that looking good won't necessarily help you to live any longer. Indeed, Barbara Cartland has lived for an extremely long time while looking absolutely dreadful. Conversely, James Dean looked wonderful and died young. It's impossible to generalise, but I'm afraid you have to do it if you want to make a case for something on the basis of very little research.
  One thing that looking good will do for you is to improve your self-esteem, which is important to the will to live. If looking in the mirror fills you with self-loathing, don't do it. Just sellotape some pictures

of good-looking people over anything reflective in your house.

But there are things that all of us can do to improve the way we look. Fashion programmes on television keenly propound the virtues of the 'make-over'. They do this by giving a dowdy, working-class housewife the star treatment with a hair-style she'll never be able to afford again, and by finding slightly overweight women to humiliate with lycra. The ethos is 'OK, you don't look like a model, but you can still make the most of what you've got'. Hence, lycra is designed to make women look as fat as possible.

Of course, looks aren't everything. Peel away Tom Cruise's skin and all you're left with is a deep feeling of satisfaction. But the phrase 'beauty is only skin deep' is not a useful one. The fact that something is only skin deep is neither here nor there. *Skin* is only skin deep, after all. There is no such thing as inner beauty; people's insides are terrible-looking things, even if they are completely healthy.

In fact, the skin can be a far more accurate indication of general health than the giblets. Having said that, looking healthy is a matter of perception. If someone has a sun-tan, their skin looks radiant with health. Of course, it is also dried, damaged and pre-cancerous, but I suppose it's a question of swings and roundabouts. For a nation of people with such an absurd pride in being *white*, it is remarkable how much time the English spend trying to turn brown – or, better still, red and scabby. An Englishman's idea of the perfect holiday is to be flat-out on a beach smothered in oil, and yet if he sees a cormorant in the same situation, it's a national emergency.[1]

Of course, the way our skin looks is also affected by

[1] I myself do not attempt to tan. I just Tippex my abdomen to make the rest of me look darker.

our eating patterns. In popular mythology, vegetarians look unhealthy. This is not because self-righteousness is bad for the complexion, but because worrying about one's diet is symptomatic of worry in general. No-one without a care in the world is likely to go out of their way to buy Quorn.

However, vegetarian food does not have to be dull. The reason it is so often boring is that it is made by vegetarians. Many vegetarians seem to believe that anything which might be regarded as a seasoning is made from crushed-up dead baby animals. So if you want to go out for a vegetarian meal and have more evidence that you are eating something than the fact that your jaw is moving up and down, you would do well to choose food from a culture whose cuisine uses spices.

Indian cooking has excellent vegetarian recipes. Unfortunately, many white English people were put off Indian food at an early age by their mothers' attempts to make curry. When I go to my favourite Indian restaurant in South London, I have a delicious savoury meal full of wonderful herbs and spices. But when my mum makes curry, a great amount of fruit seems to creep into the scenario: apples, sultanas and bananas; hundreds and thousands on the top; sponge fingers on the bottom.

Putting some fruit in your dinner seems to be the British idea of exotic. This is especially true of canteen food: they stick a pineapple ring on something and – presto – they've created Toad in the Hole Hawaiian-Style. I have to say that I am not generally in favour of putting fruit in main courses. Fruit is pudding, except for grapefruit segments with a glacé cherry on top, which is a starter. The reckless mixing of sweet and savoury flavours can only lead to monstrosities like Liver Meringue Pie.

Having said that, it's vital to experiment with food. Above all, a healthy diet is one which doesn't make you so depressed that you kill yourself. Variety is essential.[1]

It is a good idea to make recipes up as you go along because cook-book recipes are hard taskmasters. The list of ingredients for a recipe starts with mundane things like flour, eggs, meat, vegetables and margarine, to lull you into a false sense of security, but the last ingredient will be something like 'One drop of concentrated tamarind seed curd essence'. This is the one vital ingredient which gives the whole meal its unique flavour and character. It is irreplaceable, the lynchpin of the entire operation – and it is only available in twenty-litre vats from a shop on Anglesea.

So much for diet. Another part of fitness is, of course, exercise. But much of the exercise culture has more to do with looking good than feeling fit. Body-building is a prime example. Body-building will give you big muscles. But people who need big muscles, usually have them anyway, because they spend all day doing the thing they need them for. No-one whose work consists of climbing up and down ladders with hods full of bricks feels the need to unwind with two hours in the weights room. They shape up and dance with fifteen pints and a karaoke machine. Hence, weights rooms are full of the unemployed and graphic designers. The only other group who regularly do weight-training are nightclub bouncers, but even they don't need big muscles *per se*; they just need their dinner suits to be too tight. They could achieve the same effect with some cream buns and a sewing machine.

Doctors tell us that what we actually *need* in the way of exercise is to get out-of-breath three or four

---

[1]By 'variety' I don't mean selection packs of children's breakfast cereal, with names like Crispy Nut Honey Chocosmacks, which consist of delicious lumps of white sugar encrusted with tiny specks of unidentifiable toasted grain.

times a week. This means that people with asthma are extremely fit. The point of aerobic exercise is that you can judge whether you are doing enough by monitoring your breathing and your pulse. When you first take up exercise, you will only have to run around the block and you will collapse in the gutter, gasping for air, with your heartbeat dangerously accelerated. The problem arises as you persevere over a period of months, becoming gradually fitter, because it will take you longer and longer to get shagged out. So you will end up running miles and miles every day trying to get any sort of reaction out of your heart and lungs. Hence, although you may live longer, all the extra time you get is filled up with running.

Most health experts agree that the best exercise is swimming. I decided, when I first conceived of writing this lecture, that I should take up swimming, in order that I could report my progress to audiences. I joined a 'beginners adults' class at my local pool because I assumed that all the students would be at my own low level of proficiency. But, oddly, there were people in the class who could already swim adequately – nay – well. And these people were ploughing up and down the deep end, doing butterfly, which nobody can do; while crammed into the shallow end was me and about five hundred dinner ladies. It was actually obvious that they were swimmers from the moment we got changed, because they had all the state-of-the-art swimming gear: fashionable costumes, goggles, nose clips, ear plugs, water skis, harpoon guns. Meanwhile I had track-suit bottoms and plimsolls.

It is clear to me now that the sole *raison d'être* of these people is to go to lessons in things they can already do in order to humiliate genuine novices. They are probably fully competent at the whole evening-class syllabus – swimming, French, carpentry, car mainte-nance, tap, modern-sequence and ballroom – but they go along anyway just to make other people feel bad. I could achieve the same result by walking into a crèche full of toddlers and saying, 'Potato printing – bollocks. This is a fax machine.'

Friends have castigated me for my inability to swim. I have been chided with the caution that I should learn to swim because it might save my life one day. So, when I'm dying from a stab wound on the way back from the off-licence one night, I'll be kicking myself for never mastering the doggie paddle.

But here are some *useful* tips on accident prevention, which could save your life.

1: Before going to bed at night, unplug the television and video recorder and make sure you have extinguished any fires which may have broken out;

2: in the event of a fire, lie on the floor – unless the floor is on fire, in which case, lie on the sofa;

3: never leave a chip pan unattended on a railway platform;

4: chip pan fires can be extremely dangerous, although they do substantially reduce the fat content of your chips; and

5: if a fire does break out in your chip pan, don't try to put it out with lighter fluid or kindling. Simply cover yourself with a damp cloth at arm's length, retire to consider your verdict and lie in the recovery position until the ambulance arrives or Hell freezes over.

This brings me on to the subject of the Health Service. There is clearly a crisis in health care. The government believe they have identified the problem: too many hospitals. Wherever there are hospitals, there are sick people. Close down the hospitals and you get rid of the sick people. But, if there are too many hospitals, why are people dying before they get to their nearest Accident and Emergency Department? The answer must be that there are too many ambulances, cluttering up the streets and stopping the enterprising from driving themselves to hospital.

I realise that many of you are thinking that the only reason Virginia Bottomley gets away with her destruction of the Health Service is that she is the only person in the Conservative Party with whom anyone can imagine having sex. But let me explain how the internal market works and allay any fears you may have about it.

Let's imagine that you become ill. You experience pain in the lower back and difficulty in passing water. Without delay, you should consult your independent financial adviser. He will be able to tell you the kind of health insurance that's right for you; in this case, an abdomen-only policy with a shortfall hernia clause attached to a unit truss. You approach a health insurer who won't touch you because you're ill. So you then contact your GP who suspects kidney failure and phones round the local dealers to get the best price on a new kidney and the trade-in value of your old one. He accepts a bid from The Organ Works, the best-known high-street franchise transplant outlet. There's no waiting around in draughty corridors – you're taken straight in to see the consultant, who also sells you a vasectomy and a time-share in Spain. If all goes well, you'll be in and out in a day, if not, they'll dump you round the nearest Casualty where the NHS will save your life.

Of course, the best advice to anyone who wants to live for a long time is not to become ill, and, if you do contract an illness, to ensure that it's something which predominantly affects white, heterosexual males, so that you will be taken seriously. Executive stress is always a good bet. It only entails sweaty palms and wind but it's got more clout than cholera. Lower down the professional ladder, you are likely to suffer from serious stress. In fact, your employer may send you on a stress-management course, ignoring the fact that it is management who are causing you the stress.

What stress shows us is that the health of mind and body are part of a whole. If you wish to be at the height of your intellectual powers, you need to be physically fit. By the same token, if you are going to run a marathon, you've got to be mental.

A hundred years ago, psychiatric patients were treated abominably because of ignorance. Today, it's because of wilful neglect and a Tory government. But are people wrong to be insane in the modern world, or are they reacting in the only way a reasonable person can? Whatever the answer, there's not much to be said for having a complete emotional breakdown, other than the fact that it passes the time when there are engineering works at Doncaster.

This brings me neatly to the subject of *The Will to Live.* Unfortunately, that bit doesn't come next. The second part of my guide to longevity is *Stopping Other People from Killing You,* which would have followed neatly on from the bit about being stabbed on the way back from the off-licence but never mind.

Stopping Other People from Killing You

If you want to avoid being fatally injured by an *assailant*, there are all sorts of martial arts in which you can train. The trouble is that most of them are more use to violent lunatics than to people who want to be able to defend themselves. You will learn several ways of delivering a mortal blow to someone who is minding their own business, but all the throws rely on your attacker being a spiritually-attuned person in a loose-fitting white dressing gown.

So what steps could you take to deal with a potential fracas? Let's take a common scenario. You are a man having a drink in a pub. A group of other men are drinking excessively and becoming aggressive. Somehow, a conflict has arisen and a fight is about to start. What should you do? I have heard many valiant suggestions for the kind of tactics to employ in such a situation. One piece of advice I have received is 'Always hit the biggest one first'. A better idea is to buy the biggest one as many drinks as you can afford.

In short, avert the burgeoning fracas if at all possible. Choose your words carefully; the right phrase can enable you to make a humiliating climb-down without shame or embarrassment. Here are some examples of things you might like to avoid saying:

'Oh, you're very tough when there's nine of you and only one of me.'

'If you resort to violence, that just means you've lost the argument.'

'Can't you see that it's not really me you're angry with, it's yourself?'

'Could I see your warrant card please, officer.'

Try to set pride to one side. If you want to save face, take it home blushing but unbeaten. It is far better to spend your life ruefully thinking, 'Damn, if only I'd winded him with a disabling blow to the solar plexus, the other seventeen would have backed off instantly', than to actually stand up for yourself.

Men in particular can let their own aggression get them into trouble. Aggression needs to be channelled. Pent-up anger can cause us to become destructive and violent if it is not harmlessly channelled into healthy pursuits which are destructive and violent. I mentioned martial arts. There is also rugby, although it is not a purely violent sport; it also contains an element of homosexuality. Growing in popularity is American football, a version of rugby which involves wearing a lot of shelving material, holding lengthy men's encounter groups and then running a few feet every so often.

If you want to do something truly vicious, however, there are always bloodsports. I spoke to the Master of the Hounds of the East Buckinghamshire Hunt, and put it to him that many people consider fox-hunting to be barbaric. He said, 'Barbaric? Have you seen what a fox does in a chicken run?'

I replied, 'No. Have you ever seen what a pensioner does in a jumble sale?'[1]

It seems that farmers loathe vegetarianism as practised by humans and yet expect it of foxes. It's not entirely fair to blame foxes for being carnivorous. They may be cunning beasts but they haven't the wherewithal to rustle up a chickpea lasagne. The way the hunting fraternity justify their vendetta against the fox is by complaining that, when a fox gets into a chicken run, it doesn't just kill one chicken. What the fox does is to slaughter every chicken it can in a frenzy of horrifying carnage. But it's just shopping for the week. After all, if you managed to break into Safeways one night, you wouldn't think, 'Mustn't be greedy; a tin of Smedley's peas should do me nicely.'

You might now be wondering why, after these remarks, I am recommending fox-hunting as a pastime. The answer is that anyone who feels the need

---

[1] I might equally have asked him, 'Have you ever seen what a human being does in a chicken run?' We are not noted for our benevolence towards chickens. In fact, we eat their embryos, force-feed them fish meal, cut their heads off, and put their entrails into plastic bags and force them up their bottoms – none of which could be construed as charity.

to do a thing like that should spend as much time as possible galloping around rural England, maximising the chances that they will fall and break their neck.

Town-dwellers will find it less easy to engage in 'country sports'. The equivalent of fox-hunting or hare-coursing would be to go to a pet shop, buy a gerbil, take it home, break its legs and kick it round the bathroom for a few hours. Alternatively, you might be one of the growing number of enthusiasts for fighting dogs. Emotionally-stunted men half-starve dogs which have been bred and trained to kill, take them furtively to prearranged locations and then let them off the lead in children's playgrounds. When a man says, 'He won't hurt you, he's only playing,' what he means is, 'I don't have a life, so why should you?'

Even dogs which aren't vicious shit all over the place. The penalty for letting your dog foul the pavement should not be a fine. It should be that anyone who so wishes should have the right to walk into your home, any hour of the day or night, and leave a huge, steaming turd anywhere you're likely to walk.[1]

Defecating in the home of a dog-owner under the protection of the law is not only tremendous fun, but also another way of expressing one's aggression without getting into a violent situation. But it is possible that the law itself can be responsible for your death. There are still a handful of offences for which you can, in theory, be executed. Police and prison officers would like to see the return of hanging in practice, which is why they leave suicidal remand prisoners to get on with it.

But the offences for which you could legally be hanged include Treason and 'Arson in the Royal Dock-yards'. Treason covers anything from espionage to having an illicit relationship with someone in line to

---

[1] I do not like dogs.

the throne. Given that all of us have had sex with at least one member of the Royal Family at one time or another, we could all in theory find ourselves swinging from the end of a rope – if they like that sort of thing. As for the Royal Dockyards, you may, as I was, be surprised to learn that there are such things. It's hard to imagine the royals hanging around the docks. Apart from one or two of them, obviously.

Suffice it to say that there is little likelihood of the average commoner setting light to anything in a royal dockyard in the normal course of things. So you are quite unlikely to lose your life at the hands of the state. The police kill the odd person but their morale is low so I'd best not harp on about it. People are also killed by the army in highly questionable circumstances, but this is explained by their having moved their hands in such a way that it looked as though they were reaching for a gun – although how many people keep guns above their heads I don't know.

Of course, the greatest number of deaths for which the state can be responsible is in the event of all-out war. The argument for nuclear deterrence is that, if we are adequately-defended, we will not have to fight wars; but we like to have the odd one anyway to keep our hand in.

The perceived threat of war with Eastern Europe has receded, but there are always new enemies to fry. So how can the ordinary person tell if a war is in prospect? One way of telling is to look out for countries who are rearming at an alarming rate. If we're selling lots of arms to someone, you can bet we'll be at war with them in a couple of years' time.

Don't worry if all this seems a little confusing at first; once a war is under way, you'll probably find you've forgotten that our enemy was an ally three weeks ago. The important thing in terms of your own longevity is not to get involved in the fighting. Even if you are a civilian, you might still be conscripted. At one time, you could have avoided this by working in an essential industry, but the Conservatives have closed them all down so you'll have to fake poor eyesight instead. Don't bother pretending to be psychologically disturbed as this will only get you drafted into the paratroop regiment.

Of course, if the balloon really goes up, that is, if there is a nuclear war, the chances are that your life will be over before your call-up papers have even been typed. As I mentioned a moment ago, the Warsaw Pact is no more, so why do we still have nuclear weapons? The argument is that there is always the possibility that some suicidal, maniac dictator in one of the world's trouble-spots will develop the capability of making a nuclear weapon. One way of our preventing this would be by not putting the instruction leaflet in with the kit. But if he rang up and asked for it we'd be over a barrel.

All in all, if you want to avoid dying in a nuclear holocaust, you'd do well to rejoin CND and start marching for peace, although that really is something the young should be doing. If young people are going to drop acid and wear tie-died flares, they could at least riot in Grosvenor Square and make themselves useful.

Young people assume they're immortal, but the fact is that we are all going to die – or are we? Throughout history there have been individuals with an uncanny ability to defy death – the main ones being Jesus, Rasputin and Captain Scarlet. Rasputin did actually die, but only after he had survived shooting, poisoning, drowning and Bernard Matthews Mini-Kievs. Jesus cannot be killed because we killed him once and he's buggered if he's going to come back so we can do it again. Captain Scarlet, on the other hand, comes under the category of superhero. This might seem to be a glamorous way of staying alive but you do have to be very fit. Superhero status is likely to elude you if you're allergic to cheese or a martyr to your verrucas.

But not only the good die old; zombies, werewolves and vampires are also known for refusing to take death lying down. If you become one of these, there will usually be only one way in which you can be killed. However, silver bullets and stakes through the heart are not very original, and, more importantly, they are entirely feasible. You might, therefore wish to opt for something more difficult, like a banana sandwich through the skull or a hundredweight of potatoes in the trouser pocket. I should also point out that the *Living Dead* are not undead but actually dead, although this does not stop them from traipsing around graveyards in lightly soiled bandages, or shopping at Sainsbury's Homebase.

So there you are; just a few ideas for stopping other people from killing you. I shall now briefly conclude my lecture by looking at The Will to Live.

The Will to Live

This human emotion is now reckoned to have medical significance. Many doctors believe that it can add months and years to a person's life. Mind you, I lost the will to live in my early twenties and it never did me any harm.

But what have we got to live for? Sometimes it is really only the fact that we are going to die that makes us want to live. When death is staring us in the face, we might be kept going purely by our love of family, or more likely by our determination that they're not going to get their hands on our stuff. Some of us live for what is, some for what might be, others just never get round to composing their suicide note. But most of us, however appalling our circumstances might be, don't want to die. No matter how ghastly or inconsequential our lives may seem to others or ourselves, the fear that keeps our hearts pumping blood around our bodies is the fear that we might miss something. It is the same determination that made us watch *Top of the Pops* for thirty years.

Questions and Answers

As I mentioned in my introduction to this lecture, the subject touches the very core of human sensibility. For that reason, I expected some emotional contributions from the floor. Most of these were not questions but forthright opinions.

A man in Wembley Stadium, barely audible above the excited throng – there was a match on – shouted, 'I could tolerate your salacious remarks about our Royal Family, your treacherous jibes at our armed forces and your slurring of our country's good name in the field of international politics, but I cannot stand by and listen in silence while you denigrate man's best friend. Dogs gave loyal service in both world wars, and today are an invaluable asset to our unarmed and overstretched police force. And in our airports, the front line in the war against narcotics, it is dogs who are sniffing drugs on our behalf. I'd like to see some of your generation fetch a stick or dribble on my thigh when I say, "chocky drop". It is bad enough that these loyal and trusted pets are eaten by the French without them having to put up with you and your breed.'

A young man in Tossers Nite Spot in Harlech where, for some reason, I had been booked to speak as part of the entertainment for a stag night, told me, 'My gran smoked all her life. She's dead now, but she wasn't before.'

At a Weight Watchers convention in Bournemouth, an agitated woman in her late forties, shouted, 'I've lost seventeen stone!' and collapsed.

On the same theme, a student at the London College of Beauty asked, 'Do you think ladies of a heavier build are more flattered by dark colours, vertical stripes or liposuction?'

I replied, 'Designers advise that larger ladies should opt for fuller-cut concealing styles, which make the bold statement, "OK, I'm fat, but I'm ashamed." '

In a different vein, an elderly woman attending the Carlos McBogus Miracle Crusade at Olympia, where I was the support act, exhorted, 'Come to Jesus and you will receive eternal life!' This caused me some contrition, and inspired the next lecture you are about to read.

3. How To Earn Your Place in Heaven

3 How To Earn Your Place in Heaven

I was naturally delighted when Cardinal Hume asked me to deliver an Easter Sunday sermon in Westminster Cathedral. This sermon became the lecture you are about to read. I have since given it to audiences of every creed, all of whom have appreciated the profound truths within it.

First of all, what do we mean by Heaven? Before I look at the various ways in which we can try to earn a place in Heaven, I need to find a definition of Heaven which is acceptable both to atheists and to people who don't believe in God. Very few people now believe that Heaven is actually a place in the sky. We now know that the sky isn't, as early astronomers thought it to be, a line of blue crayon at the top of a sheet of paper. Nor is it a reflexion of the sea. It is in fact an illusion caused by lack of sleep. What appear to be clouds are actually electro-magnetic discharges refracting off volcanic dust particles in the earth's lower stratmosphere causing satellite television and snow. In other words, Heaven can't be somewhere in the sky because the sky isn't actually there.

So we have established that Heaven, Paradise, Valhalla, or the Happy Hunting Ground as it is known by the Royal Family, isn't a place we can see through a high-powered telescope. Nevertheless, perhaps it does exist invisibly in another dimension. Or maybe Heaven is just a lie, invented by rulers to pacify the discontented, like the Citizens Charter.

So what happens to us when we die? Well, there's usually a funeral, the purpose of which is not to remember people as they were but to try to remember them in the best possible light and hope that, if there is a Heaven, that's where they'll be. We like to think that they've gone to a better place, especially if they were from Hull. Children are told that their Gran has gone to live with the angels. 'Why do angels live at the crematorium?' the children ask.

We simply can't accept that there is no positive interpretation of death. We have to think of something cheerful to say. It was a lovely service. Wasn't it nice so many people came. The flowers were beautiful. The hearse started first time.

At the wake, we all sip sweet sherry and speak of the departed. Our memories of them conflict so wildly that we begin to wonder if we've all cremated the same person. Then we talk about dying as if it's really not such a bad thing at all; in fact we start to think the old boy should've done it years ago. And a favourite method of diminishing the tragedy of someone's passing is to say what a full life they had. But how does having a full life justify your death? I personally don't think that people should die because they've committed murder, let alone because they had a lot of hobbies.

All this studied cheer only succeeds in making death more ghastly. Funerals are depressing, there is no way round it. Even if we held them in the evening and then went on to a club, we all have to face the fact that the death of one more person we know seems to drag each of us one step nearer to the grave.

The point is, of course, that the funeral is not for the dead but for the living. So maybe we should each put more thought and planning into the kind of funeral we are going to have. Sometimes a person says that they want their funeral not to be an occasion for sadness but a joyous celebration of their life, with music and laughter and where all their friends can think of the good times and be happy. For myself, I want people's lives torn apart when I go. And it's down in my will that I'm to be embalmed and brought out when we have guests.

But the point I am struggling towards in an albeit eloquent way is that death is a hard thing to face, whether it's ours or somebody else's. So, many of us like to think that there is an afterlife. If you do believe that, you have to believe that human beings have souls – apart from bailiffs and PE teachers. If we do have souls, what happens to them when we die? Some believe that rather than go somewhere else, they turn up inside *someone* else. This is known as reincarnation. Many people claim to have been someone else in a previous existence, but it's always a famous historical figure: they never say they were a part-time cleaner at one of the pyramids or a friend of Michelangelo's brother who knew him to say hello to. You get the odd person who'll say they were a different species but even then it'll be an eagle or a dolphin, never a daddy longlegs or a slug.

Spiritualists, on the other hand, believe in a spirit world, and that they can communicate across the divide which separates the dead from the living, although we haven't heard a lot from Doris Stokes lately. There have been several feature films about spirits getting in touch with their loved ones, but is there any validity in them? Many of us greatly enjoyed the film *Ghost* but still find it very hard to believe that Patrick Swayze gets acting work at all.

So let's put spiritualism to the test. I recently obtained a Ouija board and I am going to attempt to get in touch with the manufacturers because they've put the wrong instructions in the box. I've got a board for contacting the spirit world and the rules of Kerplunk.[1]

But what is the purpose of communicating with the dead other than to tell them they've been made a high court judge? One thing we may want to know is, what's it like on the other side? Are they in Heaven? Or are they in Hell? The promise of Heaven for the saved is set against the threat of Hell for the sinner. Religion not only soothes with the prospect of happiness in the next world, it terrorises with the prospect that the next world may be far worse – unless you work in a bank.

Hamlet tells us that it is only the fear of 'The undiscovered country from whose bourn no traveller returns' that stops us all from taking our own lives. Mind you, he's a whingeing old tart, Hamlet. He goes off to university and comes back all full of Sylvia Plath and Morrissey. And what's he got to complain about? All he's got to do to avenge his father's death is to kill his uncle. It's not as if he's got to sue a hospital for medical negligence. And the worst of it is that we have to listen to all his procrastination. If he wants to put off what he's got to do, why doesn't he go and reorganise his sock drawer and leave us to get on with our ice-creams until he's ready to go through with it. And when he's finally going to do it, he can't because his uncle's praying and so would go to Heaven, unlike his dad who was murdered in his sleep before he could repent his sins. So instead of killing his uncle he has

---

[1]At the very moment I mentioned the Ouija board in Westminster Cathedral, a member of the congregation shouted, 'You are meddling with forces more evil and powerful than you can possibly imagine!' This was uncanny, how did she know that I had not bought a TV licence? This was one of countless supernatural moments in my speaking career.

a row with his mum and kills his girlfriend's dad. No
wonder they never have Danish contestants on *Family
Fortunes*.

I shall be talking about the matter of repentance
a little later but, for the moment, let's stay with
the subject of Hell and Damnation. We established earlier that Heaven is not a place in the sky,
so can we extrapolate from this that Hell is not a
place under the ground? Or is it possible that the
souls of the damned are lost and trapped for ever in
the bowels of the earth – like our nation's reserves of
coal?

The most graphic depiction of the early Christian
cosmology of Heaven and Hell is probably contained
in Milton's *Paradise Lost*, which places Heaven in the
'zenith portion' of infinite space, separated from Chaos by walls of light, and Hell in the 'nadir portion' of
Chaos on the other side of Earth from Heaven, and
linked to the Universe by a bridge built by Sin and
Death. This shows us that bugger all was spent on
scientific research in the seventeenth century, which
in turn goes to show just how long the Tories have
been in power. Anyway, as we read in Milton, Hell
was created for the defeated armies of Satan, a former
angel who had failed to overthrow God with the help
of CIA-backed contras.

So, having established what we mean by Heaven
and Hell, I shall now move on to talk about the ways
in which we can earn our place in Heaven. In general,
earning your place in heaven is about being good. I
have divided goodness into three parts:

1: Leading an entirely blameless life;
2: Doing so many good things that the bad things
   are dwarfed by comparison; and
3: Doing exactly what you like all through your
   life but repenting just in time.

Leading an Entirely Blameless Life

According to Christian teaching, it is hard to lead a blameless life because we start with a disadvantage – original sin. Babies are born bad which is why they scream all night and don't use lavatories. Baptism cleanses away this original sin with Holy Water, although baby wipes are more effective. Some Catholics still believe that the unbaptised cannot go to Heaven and instead go to somewhere called Limbo which is not the beach party it sounds but a region between Heaven and Hell where souls hover in a state of nothingness listening to Melody FM all day.

There are other Christians who think that, even if they *were* baptised as babies, they should do it again when they grow up. They believe that the first time didn't count because when they were babies they didn't agree to being baptised and had no idea what was going on. But at least they had that excuse then; it's pretty stupid behaviour for an adult. If you want to be wrapped in a sheet and have your hair washed by a stranger, go to a unisex salon. Besides, half the point of baptism is that it's a way of having a naming ceremony which isn't as violent as smashing a bottle of champagne over the baby's head. And if you've been named as a baby, you don't need to be named again, unless you've become a peer of the realm, in which case you deserve to have a bottle of champagne smashed over your head.

The idea that we are all born bad is fairly depressing and permeates much conservative thinking. Thomas Hobbes's *Leviathan* is one of the major philosophical treatises on the role of government. I haven't read it, but it's probably not very good so we don't need to worry about it.

On the other hand, William Golding's *Lord of the*

Flies is rather good but also has a very pessimistic view of human nature. A group of boys marooned on an island with no adults and no Sonic the Hedgehog get so bored and fractious that they form a right-wing paramilitary scout troop and persecute the fat, asthmatic Piggy until he falls off a cliff and dies. Whereas, if they'd had, for example, a teacher with them, he would have channelled their young energies into vigorous educational exploration. He would have organised a field trip, got them lost in a fog and they would have clung to a rockface suffering from exposure until Piggy dropped off the cliff of his own accord.

But the point Golding is making is that the beast in all of us is just below the surface, and that, when normal social constraints are removed, humans revert to being ruthless primal hunters. You may agree with this if you've ever seen pensioners in a jumble sale. On the other hand, a socialist view would be that our economic system forces individuals to put their needs before everyone else's and be ruthlessly competitive. You may also agree with *this* view if you've ever seen pensioners at a jumble sale. I'm not saying I condone their behaviour but I think it's important to understand it.[1]

But whether or not we are *born* sinful, can we go on to lead a life which is blameless after that? There are basically seven deadly sins: Pride, Gluttony, Envy, Covetousness, Sloth, Flatulence and Armed Robbery. But before something can become a sin, someone has to commit it. There's no point prohibiting something if no-one's likely to do it anyway. That's why there's nothing in the commandments about coveting your neighbour's CD of Lovejoy attempting to sing.

---

[1] In contrast to both left- and right-wing views, an anarchist analysis of jumble sales would be that it's hard to get near the trestle tables when you've got a dog on a piece of string.

We can assume, therefore, that if something has been put down on a list of sins, there are people tempted to do it. Resisting temptation is a key part of leading a blameless life. The first temptation led to the original sin. Eve was tempted by the serpent to eat of the Tree of Knowledge of Good and Evil, and she liked the fruit and so tempted Adam to eat of it, even though God had warned them that to touch the tree would mean death, because scrumping was taken very seriously in those days.

According to Genesis – by which I mean the first book of the Old Testament, not the dreadful seventies rock group which Peter Gabriel did well to leave – once Adam and Eve have eaten of the Tree, they have the knowledge of Good and Evil. This makes them realise for the first time that they are naked and so cover themselves with fig leaves. God doesn't actually kill them because they're the only two people he knows, but he does banish them from the Garden of Eden which is a bind because Adam's just put a row of tomatoes in. According to God, they must be banished lest they eat of the Tree of Life and become immortal. Having said that, I should point out that Adam does go on to live for nine hundred and thirty years, which is pretty immortal in my book.

Here is a recording made by a freelance radio reporter lucky enough to capture the temptation of Adam and Eve on tape.[1]

Serpent Eve?
Eve Bugger me, a talking snake.
Serpent Eve, hath not the Lord –

[1] I am not entirely convinced of the authenticity of this recording but the man in the pub who sold it to me seemed very nice and apparently was trying to get the coach fare back to Dunfermline together having travelled to London on the promise of a job which fell through at the last minute and his mother was ill.

Eve	Hath? What do you mean, hath?
Serpent	Don't take the pith, idth not my fault I'm a therpent.
Eve	All right, go on.
Serpent	Hath not the Lord thaid you may eat of every tree in the garden?
Eve	All except one. He says if we eat of it, we shall surely die. Something to do with pesticides, I should think.
Serpent	Yeth but he'th only thaying that becauthe if you eat of it, you will have the knowledge of good and evil and will become godth.
Eve	You mean God lied to us?
Serpent	Yep.
Eve	Bastard. Gimme some of that fruit ... Oh, that's lovely, that is. Oi, Ad! Come over here!
Adam	Bugger me, a talking rib.
Eve	Shut up and try some of this. Here, I can see your bollocks.
Adam	What bollocks?
Eve	Eat, go on.
Adam	God says we mustn't.
Eve	So, what's he going to do? Leave one of his notes? 'Will whoever it is who's been eating my fruit please buy their own?'
Adam	All right, all right. Let's have a bite ... Mmmm that's lovely. 'Ere, you haven't got any knickers on.
Eve	Bugger me!
Adam	Isn't that forbidden?
Eve	Not until *Leviticus*.

It is at this point, that Adam and Eve become self-conscious and they put the fig leaves on to cover their nakedness. You might wonder what the Knowledge of

Good and Evil has to do with getting hung up about nudity. Adam and Eve are only a few days old. Most of us don't start to become truly appalled by our naked bodies until we're over thirty. But, in any event, how might this whole ghastly situation have been avoided? Well, Eve could have refused the fruit politely but firmly with the invaluable phrase, 'Thanks but no thanks, serpent; I like forbidden fruit but I'm afraid it doesn't like me.'

So there we are; how to resist temptation without causing social embarrassment or bad feeling. But it may not only be desire that we have to watch out for. We sometimes do rash things because we've lost our temper. We can find ourselves so wound up, we just want to punch someone's face in. But we have to get a grip on our emotions, calm down, and remind ourselves that he's only a Saturday morning children's TV presenter, and he was apparently very good in *Joseph*.

Of course, our emotions would cause us less trouble if we addressed problems as they came up, instead of pretending that nothing's wrong. The English are great ones for letting a minor quibble turn into a festering forty-year grudge. We've all got an auntie who's still not speaking to another auntie because of a misunderstanding about an eccles cake during the Coronation. And a person will store up something that's bothering them until they've destroyed their family, become an alcoholic and suffered a complete nervous breakdown, and all this while trying to get Christmas Dinner on the table.

But it's not only hurting ourselves and other people we have to worry about. Nowadays, many of us try to live our lives doing as little harm as possible to the *Environment*. There are many green consumer goods on the supermarket shelves. I myself buy only biodegradable bin liners, the kind that break down naturally as you carry the rubbish down the stairs.

Instead of my old CFC-filled aerosol deodorant, I use an organic natural herbal roll-on made from coriander, which doubles as a delicious salad dressing. Indeed, some people say that they don't need to use deodorant at all, although you can usually tell that about them before they tell you.

You might also want to make sure that the make-up you buy has not been tested on animals; after all, no-one wants a lipstick with a load of dog hairs all over it. People also think much more about what they eat nowadays. Many opt for free-range chickens which have been corn-fed and humanely strangled by vegetarians.

So, there we are, just a few ideas of things you can do to lead a blameless life. A word of warning, however, moral values are relative and highly subjective, so do exercise caution when applying the principle of the Greater Good.

Doing So Many Good Things that the Bad Things are Dwarfed in Comparison

How do we set about a life of philanthropy? Well, you can start by being good to yourself. Unfortunately, that won't help anyone else much, but it's really only by learning to love yourself that you can become truly smug. Indeed, many people who dedicate their free time to helping others are extremely smug. But more about that later.

If you want to do something to help others, why not start right in your own neighbourhood? Pop in on some senior citizens and see if there's anything they need. You may not be able to give them a new hip or an income they can live on, but you can probably pick them up some fish-fingers from the corner shop.

There may also be older members of your own family who would appreciate your visiting them. Mind you, if they *did* appreciate it, they wouldn't spend the whole visit telling you that no-one ever comes to visit them.

But you may find you can help others and not even have to go out of your way to do it. Too often we close our eyes to what's going on around us. Only the other day, I witnessed an incident where people just walked on by while someone was being savagely attacked in broad daylight in a busy shopping street, and just because he'd asked his mother for an ice-cream.

And how often does a motorist think, 'Drive on, best not get involved', when a pedestrian steps on to a crossing in front of them?

There's so much we can all do in small ways to help other people. But in recent years, *charity* has become something very big. Here is an extract from one of the major fund-raising events in the TV calendar.

Presenter 1	Welcome back to Charitelly 93. Keep those telephone pledges coming in. We've got someone who used to be in Emmerdale manning the phone lines. Later on, we've got a weatherman doing something unlikely and a panto with some backbench MPs in it. But before that, over to Mike. Where are you, Mike?
Presenter 2	I'm in Carlisle in Cumbria!
(Cheers)	
Presenter 2	And I've just been handed a very generous donation from National Westmidland Bank, who've presented us with a very large cheque. It's not for much money, but it is a big cheque.

Presenter 1	Thanks, Mike! And I want to say a big hello to everyone over at the National and Commercial Building Society. They haven't given us any money at all but asked for a mention anyway, so many thanks to them. Now back to Mike. Where are you now, Mike?
Presenter 2	I'm in Stockport in Greater Manchester!

(Tumultuous cheers)

Presenter 2	And with me is a local disk jockey who is going to shave his moustache off and give all the clippings to Charitelly 93.
Presenter 1	Mike, I'm going to catch up with you later on because joining us from Westminster is the Health Secretary, Virginia Bottomley, to say a couple of words.
Mrs Bottomley	Vote Conservative.
Presenter 1	Virginia, you look absolutely lovely. Thanks for joining us. In a moment, it's back to Stockport in Greater Manchester to met our totally mad local disk jockey, but first a word about some more people who are totally mad: the mentally ill. Last year, we introduced you to Agnes. At that time, she was sleeping rough, drinking heavily and receiving no medication at all. But this year, thanks to your generosity, we've been able to give Agnes a sandwich. Now back to Mike. Where are you now, Mike?

Presenter 2	I'm in South Shields in Tyne and Weir!

(Hysterical cheers)

Presenter 1	Thanks Mike! In a moment, we'll be hearing from the winners of our Find a Theme Song for Charitelly 93 Competition, the children of St Kylie's School, Grimsby on Humberside, with their entry, 'Children of the World, Sing a New Song, to Make a New Tomorrow, For You and For Me'. But now I want you to meet a very special person: John. Now, what's wrong with you, John?
John	I'm paraplegic.
Presenter 1	That's marvellous. Now, John is one of the people who'll be helped by the money you pledge tonight to Charitelly 93. Provided he can answer these three questions. Now John, you've already got the crutches; those are yours to take home with you tonight. But if you answer these questions correctly, you could be going home in our star prize: the electric wheelchair!
John	Actually, I'm here to protest about the way your programme degrades people with special needs.
Presenter 1	Get him, boys.

Some celebrities have reputations built almost entirely upon their tireless efforts in support of charities, but as long as they're doing it, does it matter what their motives are? If they raise millions of pounds, is it right to judge them for being self-publicising egomaniacs who would rather see human beings reduced to the status of abject beggars than given their full rights in a decent society where their needs are met by the public purse and charity is consigned to the history books? If someone wants to help those less fortunate than themselves, who are we to say, 'You're a multi-millionaire; everyone's less fortunate than you, you bastard?'

And if someone wouldn't even have a career if they weren't able to go on telly and bleat on about how much they do for charity, what right do we have to tell them that they wouldn't even have a career if they weren't able to go on TV and bleat on about how much they do for charity? Ultimately, History will be their judge. Or be on a panel of judges along with Geography and French.

But these questions do raise doubts about individual acts of benevolence. What is the point in giving to charity if the government responds by spending less money on welfare and overseas aid? On the other hand, if we boycott charity, what's the betting they won't cut welfare and overseas aid anyway. It would be fascinating to get inside the head of a Tory minister. There would be so much room to stretch out.

Doing Exactly What You Like All Through Your Life but Repenting Just in Time

Our third and final ticket to a place in Heaven is Repentance. One caveat here: repentance can only earn you a place in Heaven in the literal sense of persuading God to grant you salvation, not in the metaphorical sense of being such a good person that you would deserve a place in Heaven if such a place existed. An apology might satisfy Almighty God, but it won't cut much ice with me, I'm afraid. It seems perverse to me that you can commit the most foul of crimes but enjoy eternal life if you say sorry. And it's all very well God going around forgiving people – it's never his car stereo that gets stolen.

Nonetheless, there are all sorts of people with megaphones exhorting us to repent. They usually call us 'Ye sinners' because the term 'Ye' gives a kind of historical authenticity to their claims. And they tell us that if we don't do as they suggest we'll roast in the eternal fires of damnation – which is all you need when you're trying to get the shopping done on a Saturday morning. No-one who's about to brave Tesco's on a Saturday needs to be told they're going to Hell.

And what seems strange about all this evangelising is that it's all about repenting sins once we've done them, rather than not doing them in the first place. There might be some purpose to this righteous indignation if they told people on their way into Tesco's *not* to try and pay for their shopping with an AA Relay card and not to wait until their bill's been rung up before deciding they need toilet paper.

But manic street preachers seldom specify any particular sins because they believe that we're all sinners anyway. This idea is a great leveller: it's a comforting thought that, whether you're a nose-picker or a serial killer, we're all equal in the eyes of the Lord. Even the evangelists themselves are sinners, although, to look at them, it's hard to imagine them doing anything more sinful than boring the tits off people and wasting paper.

So far I've talked about repentance as something you do once to be saved or born again. Roman Catholics, however, are supposed to repent on a weekly basis, a system of continuous assessment which seems preferable to having to remember years of sins and be tested on them all in one go. But the trouble with being a Catholic is that, even if you haven't done anything bad, you still have to confess, especially if the police are beating you up. The chances are that, from one week to the next, nothing much will happen in a person's life.

So, in Catholicism, there are extra sins, like 'Having an impure thought', which is a bit of a catch-all offence. It's hard to wake up in the morning without having an impure thought. In fact, most men wake up in an *advanced* state of impure thought. Teenage years are just one big impure thought.[1]

Of course, when we're young, we don't feel much remorse about anything. But later in life we may well

[1]Teenagers probably have more to confess than anyone else. One wonders, however, whether the parish priest is the best person to hear them unburdening their sins. In the course of my research, I took advantage of my early arrival at one of the venues for my sermon/lecture – a small Catholic Church in Liverpool – by recording an actual confession in progress. Although this was a breach of privacy, I believe it to be in the public interest. Here is the confession in full:

Girl   Bless me, Father, for I have sinned. It has been two days since my last confession.

Priest   That's not long, my child.

Girl   I know but I've got so much to tell you. See, yesterday, I skived off school and a load of us went shoplifting and then went back to Theresa's and I had eight Malibu and Pernods and Michael passed this joint round and I was sick as a dog –

Priest   My child –

Girl   and I was in Theresa's mum's bed with Michael at the time, so I had to lie to Theresa and tell her the sick was already there when we got in the bed.

Priest   If I could –

Girl   But it's all right because I don't fancy Michael anyway, because he's such a wimp. I just hate him. Honestly, I could kill him, and he's Theresa's boyfriend anyway, and Sean says I've got to pack Michael in anyway if I'm going to go out with him.

Priest   My child.

Girl   Yes, Father?

Boy   Eh, Judy, I can't undo it.

Girl   Sean, pack it in, man, I'm talking to the Father.

Priest   My child, you lead a life absolutely steeped in mortal sin. I cannot find sufficient penance. You'll have to see the bishop.

Girl   All right but tell him he's got to use a condom.

repent the excesses of youth, particularly once we're too knackered to do them any more. But it is fashionable for celebrities who are asked what they would change if they could have their lives again to reply that they would keep everything the same. Personally, I would admit to regretting certain things, like having 'Je ne regrette rien' tattooed across both buttocks.

I must also say that I feel a good deal of shame about owning an album by *Orchestral Manoeuvres in the Dark*.

So there we are: repentance – our third and final route to a place in Heaven. I wish you all the best of luck and do let me know how you get on if at all possible.

Questions and Answers

There was considerable prompting from Cardinal Hume before worshippers in Westminster Cathedral felt able to ask me anything. This was the pattern in most places of worship as congregations are not used to asking questions, and I'm afraid I did not even receive many cries of 'Halleluja, praise the Lord!' Towards the end of my tour of this lecture, I would do a bit of faith-healing just to get the audience participation going. Nonetheless, I did solicit some interesting points, both secular and spiritual, and here are some examples.

A lady at Westminster asked me, 'Do you think that the penance for venial sins is heavy enough in modern churches?'

After some thought I postulated, 'Penance is clearly not serving as a deterrent to sinners. Perhaps those confessing should lose the right to confidentiality. I suggest confessions be heard during mass and that the congregation should think up forfeits. This would have the added benefit of boosting church attendances.'

A mature student at the University of the Old Poly in Halifax confronted me with this challenge: 'You contrast sinning with doing good but the concepts of good and sin rest on bourgeois morality.'

I replied, 'Moralism is not necessarily bourgeois. I am not speaking of objective moral principles about what is right and what is wrong. I am applying *subjective*, that is, personal and emotional, moral criteria of Right and Wrong, by which I mean that I am right and you are wrong.'

He then countered, 'But the ills which attract acts of philanthropy by individuals will always exist until Capitalism is dismantled.'

I responded, 'I know that; I'm not a complete fucking idiot.'

An Anglican archdeaconness in Chester, along with many other people, asked, 'Do you believe in God?'

I replied, 'If you mean do I think that it is possible there is some kind of superhuman being in the Universe which is not a material or ethereal being but some kind of energy force, then the answer is no. If you mean do I think God is an old man with a long white beard, then the answer is yes.'

A delegate to the Police Federation conference where I was addressing a fringe meeting of Christian police officers said, 'Do you think there would be less crime if parents taught their children about Heaven and Hell?'

I replied: 'It is easier for a rich man to pass a camel than for a policeman to enter the Kingdom of Heaven, with or without a search warrant.'

He complained that I hadn't answered his question.

I said I would not answer any further questions until my solicitor arrived.

4. How To Have Sex

4 How To Have Sex

Before you read on, please be aware that, because of the subject matter, the text of this lecture contains detailed and adult discussion of downstairs things in people's front bottoms.

This talk will be in two parts, the first setting attitudes to sex in a social and historical context, and the second telling you how it's actually done.

Sex in a Social and Historical Context

It is now generally agreed that sex is not as appalling as it was once considered to be. Modern people such as myself are apt to be open-minded about the lewd and depraved things which it is possible to do with the less hygienic areas of the human body. But there is evidence to suggest that there was more openness about sex in previous millennia than there has been in the post-war period, even taking into account the 'permissive sixties'.[1]

But it was during the sixties and seventies that it began to become apparent just how sexually uninhibited the ancient civilisations were. The sudden availability of cheap foreign holidays brought an influx of postcards featuring statues of naked ancient Greek

---

[1] I don't actually remember the nineteen-sixties as being all that permissive. I was allowed to stay up for *High Chaparral* on a Monday night, but that was about it.

men in a state of arousal. For most of us, this was the first time that erect penises had popped through the letter box with the morning mail – unless we had an over-zealous postman.

Moreover, before this time we had only seen pictures of statues with erect penises in school library books, and then only because we'd drawn them on. The revelation that there are works of art which already have excited genitalia on them therefore left a whole generation of schoolboys feeling totally redundant.

Another aspect of the postcard phenomenon is that it demonstrates that a thing which is ancient will not be considered obscene. A Minoan oil lamp in the shape of an engorged winkle is considered an entirely wholesome subject for a holiday postcard, and no more lewd than a donkey wearing a straw hat. But if I made a Playdoh penis, took a polaroid of it and sent it through the post, I could be arrested – or, worse still, given a job on *That's Life*.

The Victorians, however, were no respecters of antiquity. Any sort of nudity was considered an affront. They even covered the offending portion of the Cerne Abbas Giant, the famous chalk carving in Dorset which, since being restored, has left many an archaeologist feeling hopelessly inadequate.

Nowadays, the only obscenity being carved out of the South Downs is the extension to the M3, and there is no new erotica to rival that of the ancients. There should really be a hardcore version of the *Antiques Roadshow*. For example, you may be familiar with those beautiful Japanese watercolours painted centuries ago and depicting activities which we tend to assume had never been tried before 1950. And of course, modern sex guides still refer back to the most ancient work on the art of erotic love, the *Kama Sutra*, the Sanscrit treatise which shows us that there are many more sexual positions than the four we use today: missionary, doggie fashion, man underneath and standing up in the bathroom at a party.

So, as I've suggested, there was probably a more liberal attitude to sex two thousand years ago than there is today. So what changed? In a word, Christianity, a religion which places great emphasis on virginity and celibacy. Nowadays, we know that many supposed celibates have not been as celibate as all that. In recent years, there have been many jibes at the expense of the clergy, jibes which I find personally hurtful as my own father was a Catholic priest.

Abstinence is something that has never been easy to practise, as becomes apparent when we read the visions of the early saints. Here is an extract from the Revelation of St Dolores of Athlone which dates back to the tenth century:

> And all was darkness and I did sleep, and in my sleep a dream the Lord did visit upon me. A great burning was about my loins and an angel of the Lord appeared. And I saw that he was poor for only a loin cloth did he have. And his loin cloth he removed and lo he was hung. And I knew him to be Samson of old for, 'My, my, my Delilah' did he sing. And I saw that he was lame for a mighty staff he carried. And I spake and said, 'Wilt thou not rest? I have but a rude bed of straw but I will it share, and your rude staff safely stow in a place which is warm.' But, alas, Satan was abroad and he did blight the staff and it did wither to an tiny stem and the angel spake and said, 'I'm sorry, this doesn't normally happen to me.'

Sexual repression probably reached its peak in the nineteenth century. For the Victorians, sex would seem to have consisted of a married couple lying fully-clothed in separate rooms while doctors poured boiling water over their privates and recited Tennyson.

The only publicly acknowledged reason for having sex was so that a woman could conceive – and preferably die in childbirth.

Of course, on the quiet, the Victorians were up to all sorts of things. A Victorian gentleman would spend the day lamenting the moral laxity of the poor and organising missionary expeditions to force the Massai tribe to wear underpants, and at night would go out cruising the slums, hiring chimney sweeps to dress him up as a shepherdess and sodomise him with a bust of Palmerston.

Today we are quite used to the idea of private vice and public virtue, as it is now much harder for people not to get caught. Indeed, one often suspects that those in high places are actually quite keen to get caught. It was the making of Paddy Ashdown to be revealed as an adulterer. Rather than bewail the hurt and humiliation he had caused his family, he seemed to strut around like a Jack Russell who's just mated with a French poodle. A sex scandal can do wonders for your public image. I don't know whether the John Major stories were true or false, but he'd have done well to cultivate them rather than use them to bankrupt a left-wing magazine. The idea that somebody finds John Major sexually attractive would surely have done him no end of good.

These days it is not only the sex lives of politicians which can become public property. If you're sat around at home, you can dial an 0898 number and talk filth with one of the Royal Family any hour of the day or night. A tremendous change has taken place in our assumptions about sex and the monarchy. At the time when Her Majesty the Queen was conceiving her now-libidinous children, not only was it not imagined that they would ever grow up to be fornicators, it was not even imagined that she had conceived them by any other means than the will of God. Today, however,

if someone released a video of a porn film she made
early on in her career, no-one would be particularly
outraged.

So when did the great relaxation begin? The Second
World War is often credited with playing a major part
in the sexual liberation of women. There is a very
clear sociological reason for this, which has to do
with chewing gum, munitions factories, eye pencil
down the back of the leg and that. But the great
period of sexual exploration was the fifties, the era of
big suits, capuccino, affluence and ponytails – oh, no,
sorry, that was the eighties. But, above all, the fifties
saw the birth of Rock 'n' Roll. The beat was a hard-
driving fusion of black R&B and white plagiarism, and
the music had an overtly sexual rhythm and message,
apart from Bill Haley, obviously.

After the fifties came the sixties and *Lady Chatter-
ley's Lover* was published which was a major blow
against literary censorship, although the only people
who have any interest in the works of D.H. Lawrence
are teenage boys who fantasise about having sex with
ploughed fields. Then it was the *Oz* trial; then the seventies when all the music for porn films was recorded,
and we saw a lot of Frank Finlay with sideburns doing
it on the telly; then it was the eighties when, if you
suggested sex to someone, they said, 'Leave it with
me, I'll have to get back to you on that'; and now it's
the nineties.

In the nineties, people are starting to be promiscu-
ous again. The public can be very fickle in the matters
about which they show concern. Five years ago, people were putting condoms on to watch *The Holiday
Programme*, but now they seem to think they're safe
from AIDS as long as they've got a plastic squashed
tomato tied to the front of their car. The condom is
not a popular device. Having sex using a condom has
been described by countless wags as being 'like having

a bath with your clothes on'. The trouble is that having sex without using a condom is like having a bath with a three-bar electric fire.

One group, however, who have no use for condoms and are at very little risk from HIV are, of course, lesbians. All in all, it's a good time to be a lesbian: sex is safe, kd lang is a success; and young men are all wearing hooded baby clothes so you wouldn't want to be seen out with one anyway. Moreover, women are much better at sex than men. Therefore, it follows that, if you are a woman, the best person with whom to have sex would be another woman. Call me old-fashioned if you like, but that's what I think.

I believe women to be better at sex than men because they are so much nicer about it than we are. Women are by far the more supportive and encouraging sex. They tell us things like, 'Look it doesn't matter. I don't mind, really. We can still have a nice time, even if you did lose your genitals in a lift door.'

Having argued that women should be lesbians, I must warn any women who are thinking of following my advice that you will face considerable prejudice. There's many a man who resents lesbians for not wanting to go to bed with him, completely ignoring the fact that, even if they weren't lesbians, there's every chance that they still wouldn't want to go to bed with him – and would, therefore, by his own definition, be lesbians.

How It's Actually Done

So, having set sex in its historical and social context, I shall now explain how to *have* sex. One of the most frequent complaints I hear about people's relationships is, 'If only he was more like you, Jeremy.' Another all-too familiar complaint is that sex is all over so quickly. My advice is to start a bit later. This will mean drinking a lot more coffee.

Crass though the Gold Blend television advertisements may have been, they have latched on to the important correlation between sex and coffee. In the first commercial of the series, which was many years ago now, the male protagonist was at home and his new neighbour arrived saying, 'Hello, I've just moved in and I seem to have run out of coffee, and there's an awful lot of middle-class people in my living room. So, I wondered if I might borrow some coffee with a view to our having sexual intercourse at some point in the future.'

We use coffee to put off the moment of sexual proposition. In the case of the Gold Blend couple, for about two and a half years. By the time that we could safely draw the inference that penetration had occurred, this once-glamorous couple were looking rather decrepit. This raises another issue.

For a long time it was assumed that the elderly were post-sexual beings. Now there is hardly a sitcom on the television which does not feature old people trying to mount each other at every possible opportunity. It is true that the old are still capable of enjoying the heated passion of writhing entangled bodies as clothes are ripped off in an orgy of self-gratification – as you'll know if you've ever seen pensioners at a jumble sale.[1] So why do the rest of us feel slightly uncomfortable about the idea of older people making love? It may be that we cannot imagine ourselves in that situation. Or it may be that we resent the fact that old people have so much time on their hands they're probably doing it more than we are.

---

[1] The reader will have observed that this is something of a theme in my lectures.

There is also squeamishness about the fact of people with disabilities having sex. They are expected to just sit around playing ping-pong and feeling grateful to Telethon. It would be an occasion of great joy if the presenter of one of those TV charity galas said, 'And now let's look at some of the people you're helping tonight,' and the cameras cut to a couple having vigorous sex in a wheelchair saying, 'No thanks, we don't need any help at the moment.'

Surely the reason why the thought of other people doing it is repellent to us is that they do not fit our own fantasy of the perfect body. The mythology of sex involves only beings of perfection. People whose jeans fit like clingfilm. Whose stomachs point inwards. Whose legs are never blotchy. Who can toss their hair without things falling out of it. Who can let ice-cream run down their chins and look like love-gods instead of messy herberts.

Sex is idealised by film and literature. Lovers in fiction are prepared for sex at all times. They never have to use birth control. They never have to go to the bathroom before sex to make sure the relevant bits aren't too smelly to do it with. They never have to stop half way through to go to the lavatory. They always finish in time with the music, and they always finish together. It is one of the great mysteries of anthropology that people are expected to climax at the same time. Why should they? After all, they don't sneeze at the same time.

Sex is supposed to happen according to the precepts of text books and any discrepancies be ironed out by technique. Here is the introduction to one of the best-selling educational sex guide videos.

Woman   Hello and welcome to the Lovemakers' Guide to better love-making. I'm Doctor Anthea Clitoris, a specialist in Neuro-

	Sexualogical Made-Upology at the Hospital for Eroto-Psychomaniac Disorders, Coventry.
Man	And I'm Professor Victor Love-Thing of the Department of Hold-On-Baby-Oh-Yes-Do-It-To-Me-Now-One-Time Studies at the University of Sex, Coventry, Illinois.
Woman	In the course of our work as psycho-scatalogical neurotic counsellors, we meet many people, who ask us questions like, 'Doctor, is it true that an erection can alter the line of my trousers?'
Man	'Professor, can death affect male potency?'
Woman	'Doctor, are small breasts just as good?'
Man	And, 'Professor, can women enjoy sex too?'
Woman	How we feel about ourselves is important.
Man	So we've produced this video for people who want to feel about themselves.
Woman	But it's also important to feel *good* about yourself. Men often worry that their penises are too small, but we can reassure you that all penises are exactly the same size, except for yours which is bigger.
Man	And now we're going to meet Gino and Helga, a normal happily married couple who don't mind having sex in front of a film crew for four days.

A video cannot help you to have sex, except with yourself. Some degree of sexual technique can be beneficial, however; if someone says, 'Was what all right for me?' you may be on the wrong track.

But there are extremes. One reads about the painstaking efforts of couples to prolong and heighten the intensity of their ecstasy: just before the moment of climax, the man will withdraw and hit himself in the testicles with a hammer.

Women's magazines – that is, the fashionable, glossy magazines for independent, go-ahead, confident women – revolve entirely around men. They have headlines like, 'Is your man a real man?', to which the only possible answer is, 'Well, he can't be a hologram because he can catch peanuts in his mouth.'

These magazines also feature many articles about orgasms. There will be 'Orgasms and Tax', 'Orgasms for the Self-Employed', 'Orgasms and Starting Your Own Business'. I even found one in the course of my research about the male orgasm. This article said that it had been discovered that men can have multiple orgasms too. The word 'too' seems to suggest that the author of the piece believes there to be people other than men who have multiple orgasms. These people, I assume, are women.

I am by no means an expert on female sexuality, but from what I can gather, a multiple orgasm is like a good stereo – something you see in magazines and which other people have. You may have thought you had one, but it was probably hiccups. And I should point out that, when I say 'multiple orgasms', I don't mean several over a period of years.

It is, in any case, foolhardy to tell men that there is still more to be gleaned from sex, because men always want more from sex. Men seeing that article will have asked their partners, 'Why can't I have a multiple orgasm?' and their partner will have replied, 'We've been through all this. The flat's too small and it would make too much mess.' And a couple who have just achieved simultaneous orgasm after years of practice will now feel obliged to have eight or nine orgasms each, all at the same time, and if one of them has too many the whole evening's been a total disaster.

It is no wonder that most people can't face sex until

last thing at night. Which is a shame. At our level of social sophistication, we should really be able to make love when we feel like it, public transport permitting. Instead we relegate sex, postpone it so that it is just one last grisly chore to struggle through before we can go to sleep. Our attitude to sex is, 'Well, we're lying down anyway, we might as well give it a try.' On the other hand, if we have an early night, it's over by about five past ten and we've got to get up again and watch telly, or make it down the pub for last orders.

Of course, according to pulp fiction, human beings make love all night. Here is a paragraph from *Riders on the Ground* by Lucy de Krepitte:

> We made love all night and, as the sun cast its first golden rays on to the dunes our bodies were still intertwined in a togetherness of bodies seemingly intertwined. We breathed as if to draw in air, air which had been pounded from our bodies during our endless pleasure which seemed never to end in its seeming endlessness which seemed to be an eternity as it finally ended. It ended in a crescendo of finishingness which seemed to last for ever.[1]

That is unlikely to bear much resemblance to your sex life, unless you are in a new relationship. In that exciting circumstance, when your love is a voyage of discovery, you may indeed spend whole nights having sex. But there is a price to be paid. What you fail to realise is that you are using up your goes.

So what can you do to keep alive the passion in a sexual relationship? Above all, the important thing is to *listen*. Many of us don't listen to our sexual partner,

---

[1] I used to read more or less of this passage, depending on the audience. At some girls' boarding schools, I was forced to read seven or eight Lucy de Krepitte novels before order could be restored by the staff.

because they make such stupid noises that we'd laugh if we did. It is important, however, to tell your partner what you want – unless it's sex with someone else or a different species. Role-playing can also be helpful. For example, I play the part of Gwendolen in *The Importance of Being Earnest*, while my wife re-enacts beach landings from *The Battle of Midway*. Love-making should be about play and experimentation, so get the Scrabble out and cut up a few rats.

But I'm jumping ahead here. Before any of this happens, you've got to find someone to do it with. So what kind of person should you look for? I've already suggested that women might want to look for someone of the same sex, but what about men?

Male homosexuality inspires even more wrath than lesbianism, and there are also more legal restraints upon it. It is often cited that Queen Victoria would not agree to the banning of lesbianism because she would not believe that any woman would do it. I'm bound to say that I don't believe that anyone would shoplift Bernard Matthews Golden Drummers but you can still go to prison for it.

On the other hand, Queen Victoria's logic has spared lesbians much of the legal discrimination which confronts gay men. The age of consent for gay men is twenty-one, which is preposterous when you consider that men reach their sexual peak at seventeen. It is rather like not letting people take their driving test until they're seventy-nine. And homosexuals are not allowed to join the Army, because armies involve the intimacy of large numbers of men being together all the time, sleeping in tents and having showers together. All this means it's a bit pointless joining up if you're *not* a homosexual.

Both gay men and lesbians are widely considered to be unsuitable for teaching posts, because parents are worried that their children will be influenced. These fears are groundless. If children emulated their teachers' lifestyles, my whole generation would be wearing corduroy jackets with elbow patches.

I canvassed a wide range of opinions about sexuality before composing this lecture. One frequent complaint about gay men was, 'Why do some of them find it necessary to go into toilets to pick each other up?' I suggested that it was for the same reason that people find it necessary to go into toilets to urinate: they're not allowed to do it anywhere else. If people were not inhibited from relieving themselves in W.H. Smith, they would. I'm sure most of us would much rather pop behind the Easy Listening display for a slash than go into some dingy old lavatory and interrupt a lot of people who are trying to get off with each other.

But, for those who want more than a casual encounter, you are unlikely to form a meaningful relationship in a toilet. So if you live in Wolverhampton, you'd do well to move. Actually, there are now quite a lot of gay pubs and clubs where you can go to meet other gays. This fact inspired resentment among some of those people I questioned: 'How come there are special clubs for gays but not for heterosexuals?' they would protest. The fact is, of course, that there are clubs for heterosexuals, even though they are not advertised as such. A club called Valentino's of Didcot might trumpet the fact that ladies get in free on Thursdays, but the management would be very disconcerted if the ladies showed up in pairs.

Most organised social activities are dedicated in some way to heterosexuality. There are even heterosexual package holidays so that young people with highlights and low reading ages can have unprotected sex on foreign soil. Colleges have all sorts of clubs and societies, and the Gay Society is likely to be far-exceeded in terms of carnal activity by both the Christian Union and the Federation of Conservative

Students, even though they have extremely ugly memberships.

Universities also have an annual heterosexual orgy for people who went to private schools. This is known as the May Ball and it entails a male student buying two very expensive tickets, one for himself and one for a woman, who is to accompany him wearing a ball-gown cut for the kind of cleavage which only exists in Renaissance art. At the Ball, the couple eat a meal, become very drunk and dance feebly to a retired jazz band, after which the man is sick in his cummerbund and the woman gets off with someone else.

What we can conclude from all this is that, whatever your sexuality, trying to find someone to have sex with can be a dispiriting business. And many of us set our sights rather high. For example, people advertising in the personal columns of magazines can be extremely particular about the kind of partner they are seeking. Here are two examples:

> Attractive woman, 30, seeks gentle, funny, athletic, multi-lingual, vegan man, who likes cats that stink and live-in grandparents, for laughs, long walks, cuddles and understanding of suicide attempts. Graduate preferred. Must have own car and powers of levitation. Photo please, no one-nighters.

> Older man (58) of not repellent appearance, interested in conveyancing and British wines, seeks property-owning, non-smoking female, 17–18, with private income and access to weapons grade plutonium, for marriage with a view to long-term nursing care. Nude photo please, no Catholics.

Despite your obvious revulsion at that man's advertisement, I am sorry to say that he is the more likely of the two to be successful in his quest. It is extremely common for perfectly nice and attractive women to end up with revolting men. Obviously, as a man, I am biased in this regard. Whenever a man sees a beautiful woman, he looks at her partner and thinks, 'What's she doing with that bastard?' and decides that he is either rich, her pimp, or an evil scientist who has brainwashed her and is keeping her prisoner. In fact, whenever I see a happy young couple canoodling in the park on a summer's day, I want to run over, kick the man vigorously in the pelvis and say, 'Don't worry, miss. This creep won't bother you any more.'

Having said that, I can also say, quite dispassionately, that in my younger days I knew several beautiful and wonderful women who ended up with total reptiles when they should have ended up with me. I have concluded that, because men are frightened of women, and especially of beautiful women, only those men who are so arrogant and myopic that they have no idea what an appalling piece of slime they are have the courage to approach stunning goddesses of beauty. While the rest of us assume that we're only fit to fill the role of platonic, nebbisch brother-figure, who hangs around ready to be a shoulder to cry on when Lover Boy turns out to be a sadistic, foul-smelling arms dealer with 666 written behind his ear.[1]

But how does a woman get the man she wants? If you are a woman, and you think you've met Mr Right, you need to beguile him with your subtle, feminine wiles, by suggesting immediate sex. In general, whatever your sex or sexuality, how you act when you meet someone is the most significant factor. It is the old confidence trick of playing dead while you stare out a shark who comes sniffing around your tent. If someone acts as though

---

[1] On reflection, I think I allowed my own emotions to somewhat cloud this issue.

they are attractive, clever and interesting, we assume that they must be, and that our impression that they are in fact an arsehole must be wrong.

So it is all about confidence. Avoid an opening gambit like, 'Hello, you won't have noticed me but I've been following you around for weeks and sleeping on your mother's grave just to be nearer to you.' There is nothing less appealing than throwing yourself on someone's mercy or appearing desperate. Phrases like, 'Oh go on' or 'Everyone always says that' are of little use in terms of their seductive power.

Of course, these days most of us are quite wary of meeting someone and having sex straight away. It is more likely that you will wish to take things one step at a time. One final note of caution here, however. If you wait too long, you'll find that you have become friends, and one of you won't want to do it. It is one of the ironies of our existence that the more you know, trust and like someone, the less likely you are to leap around naked with them. For some reason, a friend can come over to your house, get completely drunk, need to stay the night, throw up over your sofa and steal some money in the morning, and you'll be buddies for life. But if instead of doing that they come round and make love with you, it puts a terrible strain on your friendship.

Questions and Answers

As you might expect, hundreds of people were eager to benefit from my advice on sexual matters, although some of my practical demonstrations were stopped by plain-clothes police officers. I was actually arrested on the Isle of Wight, but normally a policeman would just give me a caution and his phone number. I wish I could tell the reader about all the questions I received but many of them were obscene and involved household hints on stain removal. I would also add that, although my advice was freely given on these occasions, I am not able to enter into private correspondence about sexual problems because, like any agony aunt, I don't care that much.

A worried mother in Glasgow asked me, 'Mr Hardy, my son is fifteen and spends all day in his room playing video games. Shouldn't he have started masturbating by now?'

I set her mind at rest: 'There is no right age to start having sex with oneself. If he respects himself, he will allow himself to wait until he's ready. The fact that any sane and healthy child would have started at around three should not worry you.'

A fifteen-year-old boy at St Nintendo's School in Bury where I was a guest of honour at Speech Day, asked, 'Do you think that Virtual Reality will replace sex?'

I answered, 'Probably, but it'll never replace masturbation.'

Another boy asked, 'Does this look normal to you?' and was instantly expelled.

A man at Pontardawe Community Centre, near Swansea asked, 'Do you think that we are all bisexual?'

I phrased my answer very carefully. 'I think that women have the potential for heterosexual and homosexual relationships. Men will just fuck anything.'

A man at the Runfold Village Fête in Surrey, where I had been asked to say a few words before the raffle, said, 'Mr Hardy, my wife doesn't like fellatio.'

I reassured him, 'It's just as well she hasn't got a penis then, isn't it?'

The wife of a local Conservative councillor then complained, 'My husband insists on anal sex. I find it unpleasant and painful. How can I get him to stop pestering me about it.'

I advised her to take several laxatives and then accede to his demands.

Many people of all ages and both sexes, all over the country, were worried about the fact that they had never had sex. I usually told them, 'Having sex may be very satisfying, but there is no satisfaction in having *had* sex, except for about half an hour. Therefore, most of the time you're no worse off than anyone else, except that *they're* resting on their laurels and *you're* worried that your laurels have never been rested on. And since you probably eat much more chocolate than other people, you're probably happier than they are anyway.'

5. How To Know Your Place

5 How To Know Your Place

The issue of class causes more argument than anything else, to paraphrase Marxist theory. I cannot say that this lecture incited civil disturbances or the setting up of workers soviets, but it certainly provoked some lively discussions.

During the course of this lecture, I shall be looking at the Great British obsession: Class. I shall be asking the question, 'Is Britain still a class society?' And I shall be answering, 'Yes, of course it is, obviously. What kind of question is that?' So what is class? Well, according to the *Concise Oxford Dictionary*, the definition of class is: 'Device for fastening things, with interlocking parts, handshake or embrace.'[1]

People often compare Britain unfavourably to America when it comes to class. The United States seems to be a much more meritocratic society. We can see this in the professionalism of its institutions. Take the secret service. The CIA is able to destabilise countries and organise right-wing death squads, whereas MI5 is run by those Oxbridge graduates who are too dimwitted to get their own TV series.

Even within Britain, institutions vary in the extent to which class is a factor in recruitment. Look at the army. To be in the Brigade of Guards you've got to come from the right background, but to be in the

[1] I now realise that, in copying from my dictionary, I had mistakenly written down the definition of 'clasp'.

SAS you've just got to be the right man for the job, wherever you came from. The Guards can afford to put breeding before ability because the job consists mainly of camping it up in funny costumes outside Buckingham Palace. But the SAS demands more. It's no easy thing to look a man in the eye while you pull the trigger, especially if he's lying face down on the ground.

But even in our class-ridden society, a person does not necessarily stay in the same social class into which he or she was born. While it is still the case that the majority of senior civil servants, high court judges and Conservative MPs have received a private education – an education so private that very few of them have any idea what's going on in the world – there are always exceptions.

Theoretically, in a free market economy, there's nothing to stop a poor black child in Notting Hill from one day driving a Rolls Royce. Of course, there'd be no point because he'd be stopped by the police every four or five feet, but in theory he could do it.

And look at my own class origins. I was born on a council estate, but when I was a year old, my parents bought a little bungalow in suburban Surrey. Surrey is not known for social deprivation. If any kids went barefoot down our street it was because their parents put Wilton carpet outside on the pavement. My father was from a poor background and was fiercely proud of owning his first home. He kept asking people in to use the toilet just because it was indoors. And we were the only Labour family in the whole street, because Surrey is, to say the least, a Conservative stronghold. In fact, I can remember Methodists being hunted for sport right into the 1960s.

But the Conservative Party is itself an interesting study in social mobility. Both our last two prime ministers had inauspicious beginnings. Lady Thatcher was a humble grocer's daughter who rose to the highest office in the land, having married a millionaire.[1] And John Major is a self-made man. Indeed, he looks as if he got himself in kit-form, and couldn't quite read the instructions properly.

When Mr Major became prime minister in 1990, he said his aim was to bring about a classless society by the year 2000. It is now 1993, and there doesn't seem to have been much progress. He's got to have the Revolution, the Dictatorship of the Proletariat, the Gradual Withering of the State and the Evolution into a Classless Society all in seven years. The man is a hopeless communist dreamer.

Mr Major has been very keen to play up his working-class image. In legend, before he became prime minister, he was just an ordinary, salt-of-the-earth, working-class bloke, although, to be fair, he had been Chancellor of the Exchequer, not a cockney chimney sweep. In this regard he's about as credible as Dick Van Dyke in *Mary Poppins*. And yet, during the general election, much was made of his ordinary background. And he went down to Brixton in South London, the deprived inner city area where he had once lived, and went to the market to buy a fish – or so he waned us to believe. This is a man who's running a country, fighting an election, and lives right in the middle of town with excellent shopping facilities and a whole staff of people able to nip out and buy him a fish if he's desperate. Why does he go all the way to Brixton? To buy a fish? No, to buy one thing and one thing only: drugs. That's why the cabinet members look so glazed all the time.

What Major seeks to do is not to convince us that his present occupation is working-class but that his *tastes*

[1]In retrospect, that is a cynical remark, Margaret Thatcher may not have married Denis for his money. It might have been his looks, his charisma or his intelligence.

are.[1] You've probably jumped ahead of me and are thinking that what clouds the issue of class more than anything else is the fact that so many commentators on the subject have been seduced by the lifestyle-oriented Weberian branch of western sociology. Most modern sociology derives from the theories of Max Weber, the German Social Democrat who believed that the best way to oppose Marxism was to clutter class theory up with issues like how people pronounce 'croissant' and how many sugars they have in their tea.

Marx's analysis, on the other hand, is all about economics. He defined the principal social classes as the *boulangerie* and the *profiteroles*, with the *petit déjeuner* in between. In Marxist theory, there is an irresolvable conflict between the interests of the people who do all the work, have no money and no power and no control over their lives, and the people who have all the money and power, own and run everything and exploit the other people. But of course a lot has changed since Marx's day. Stamps have gone up, for example.

But again we come up against the problem of definition. A Marxist definition of the working class would include all those people who live purely by the sale of their own labour and are not involved in the extraction of labour from others. But other class analysts would use 'working-class' to define only blue-collar workers, and would include white-collar workers in the middle class. If one wished to wax poetic, one might say that as long as workers are kept on a leash it does not matter what colour their collar is. If all office staff are middle-class, you can be torpefied by air-conditioning, deprived of natural light, and half-deformed from being hunched over a keyboard all day, but so long as there's a dead pot-plant and a jokey noticeboard in the workplace,

[1] If Mr Major really wants working-class credentials, he should get the cabinet off dope and on to crack.

you're in the same social stratum as senior management.

Many would say that if a person cannot be easily classified as working-class *or* middle-class, then a useful term is *lower-middle-class*. But this is not a term which should be used lightly. The main characteristic of the lower middle class is that they may not have very much but will fight to the death to defend it. Such people form the backbone of fascism. The visible face of fascism is made up of those scary-looking men with little hair who have a flair for violence but difficulty in using a spoon. But these are not the ideologues, they are simply people who passionately believe what other people tell them. The people doing the telling, the driving force behind fascism, are the people who've worked all their lives to own an ailing small business and some patio doors which no left-handed, pot-smoking asylum-seeker is going to be allowed to take away from them.

Because lower-middle-class people are physically nondescript, they are not readily identifiable. You will find them at neighbourhood watch meetings, which I'm not knocking necessarily; if you want to learn German, it's as good a way as any. But it is only when speaking to these people that you realise how frightening they truly are. For example, they read the *Daily Mail* because they think it is a good newspaper; they do not wish their children to be educated alongside Asian children because, although they're not being funny, they're worried that their children might pick up alien Indian customs, like drinking tea and eating chutney; and when you meet them on holiday, they say, 'We must keep in touch' and, terrifyingly, they do. Of course, the only reason that they have a foreign holiday is so that they can have an appalling time and be glad to come home.

We have established that 'lower-middle-class' is not so much a social definition as a term of abuse, but what of the middle class as a whole? Who are the middle class, and what do I mean by 'middle-class'? Am I talking about our relationship to the means of production or our lifestyle? Am I talking about status or income? What am I talking about?

Oh yes, I remember. Often when people speak of class, they mean status. And a higher status does not automatically mean a higher income. A trained professional, like a teacher, might earn less than someone unskilled and with low status, like a journalist. Solicitors have high status and are regarded as solidly middle-class, but if they do legal aid work they may earn less than old ladies who put paper clips in boxes. On the other hand, a manager might earn more than Princess Margaret gets in fag money but would still only be 'upper-middle-class', not 'upper-class'.

This is because, by 'the Upper Class', we generally mean the aristocracy, our hereditary social élite. In this country, one can simply inherit the kind of titles which in America are reserved for only the most respected jazz musicians. I spoke to many of our biggest landowners as part of my research for this subject, and, interestingly, I found that all of them tend to deny the very existence of Class. A good example was Lord 'Jock' Aberlaird, Fourteenth Earl of Strathbannock, who spoke to me in his ninety-roomed mansion in Aberdeenshire. These are his words:

> Now look, I'm a typical earthy Scotsman, as you can hear from my English accent, and I'm so tired of you media types bellyaching on about this class business. I was saying how outmoded it is only the other day in my speech to the Lord Lieutenant's charity bear-baiting banquet. You see, what you don't understand is that my enormous wealth is more of a curse than a blessing. I can't leave the estate. If I went off on a world cruise,

who'd look after the dogs – apart from the servants? I have to preserve my inheritance for the nation. We've got one of the finest collections of antique agricultural injuries in the shire. And I'm just an ordinary bloke like any other. I go down to the village and I feel perfectly at home. Well, I suppose it is my home. I do own it. And I sit down in the pub for a good honest pint with the ghillies and they regard me as being just like one of them. Only much, much richer. And with my own brewery. And come harvest time, I think nothing of rolling up my sleeves and ringing the farm manager for a jolly good natter. I mean, I know I've got some defects, and some of them have been in the family for generations. But I got my wealth through honest labour, my mother gave birth and that was it. And, frankly, I envy the working man. He gets a wage packet at the end of every week; but if you inherit your money, you get it all in one go and that's your lot.

What we call *old money* is still very influential in Britain. A dynasty based on *new money*, that is, created wealth, will take generations to be assimilated by the aristocracy, although rock stars over forty are accepted unconditionally. Old money is very important in the City and in industry, but its owners still rather look down upon 'trade'. No matter how rich a capitalist has *become*, the suspicion that his grandfather may have been a tailor in Lithuania does not sit well with the upper classes. Furthermore, the new-money whizz kids of the Thatcher revolution are despised by old families for being brash, vulgar, ruthless philistines. Actually they are, but that's not the point. The reason why the upper classes think that is that effort is not considered gentlemanly, except on the field of play. Gentlefolk are not professionals – they dabble. Gentlefolk have nothing to prove; they have an inborn grace which comes from centuries of careful breeding. Like pedigree dogs, they are pure, sleek, elegant and unable to get their own dinner.

You might think that I'm exaggerating our society's belief in the divine right of toffs, but how else can one explain the fact that hereditary peers sit in the House of Lords? Crucial examination of important legislation is left to people barely able to keep track of their own saliva. And there must be a belief that some people are just born lovely because, as well as an aristocracy, we have a monarchy.

Royalty have enjoyed widespread supplication by the populace for generations, but more and more people are now saying that the time has come to put them out to grass. The last time we got rid of the monarchy was when we executed Charles I. Very few people think we should actually cut the Royal Family's heads off. Some of us don't think it would change them very much. But admirers of the royals tell us that they work very hard for this country. It's true that they do a great deal for tourism; they're always on holiday.

More importantly, it is often said that the monarchy is a useful constitutional device because, although the Queen is Head of State, she has no real power. But she's got a fair bit more than most of us. After an election, it is the Queen who calls upon someone to form a government. True, she has no say in who it is, but you'd think in John Major's case she'd at least have tried to stall him for as long as possible – steer the conversation on to something else. She could have taken him for a stroll around the garden; it is enormous. She could have taken him all around the palace and shown him where Philip is thinking of knocking through, into South London.

If Arthur Scargill were elected prime minister, she'd be shouting through the letter box at the palace saying, 'They're not here. They've moved. I don't know where they are. We're just squatters.' And if Her Majesty is above politics, how is that, when standing before both Houses of Parliament to deliver the annual Queen's Speech, she doesn't say, 'I'm sorry, John, I just can't read any more of this bollocks?'

Over the last few years, the Queen has tried to appear more socially responsible. For example, she instructed that all the royal cars must use lead-free petrol – as soon as she found out you have to put petrol in cars. I'm sure she felt mightily aggrieved when she realised the chauffeur had been pocketing all the free tumblers for years. And more recently it was announced that the Queen wants to pay tax. Of course, she doesn't want to pay tax. No-one *wants* to pay tax. The only reason any of us pay it is that we're afraid that if we don't, people will come and take all our stuff away. And in her case it would be us.

It could not have been a coincidence that the announcement was made shortly after the Queen's house burnt down and no-one cared. I say 'her house', but it's not as if she didn't have several others to choose from. She didn't have to spend the weekend with neighbours.

And one wonders how successful was the bid to turn Prince Andrew into the David Hasselhoff of fire, rushing in to save valuable paintings from the inferno. I suspect that Prince Andrew was the wrong person to be salvaging national art treasures, anyway. He probably rescued two Garfield posters and a waste-paper basket.

But I digress. The point I am attempting to make is that the Windsors probably hoped that, in the aftermath of the fire, a wave of public sympathy would sweep them back to their position as Britain's favourite family. But it seems that their subjects are no longer as happy to be subjects as they used to be. So should we have a presidency? If so, we must address the issue of whether the president should have governmental power or merely be a figurehead.

Perhaps there is, after all, an advantage in having a Head of State who is not identified with any political viewpoint – someone from the Labour Party, for example.

When it was founded, the Labour Party was intended to represent the working class. But nowadays, experts in style and communication advise that the party needs to shed its working-class image because, they say, the working class is no more. If it is true that Britain no longer has a working class, it follows that we must ask, 'Who's emptying the bins then?' But the fashionable view among those people who wish to drag the Labour Party ever further to the right is that the working class has been absorbed by the middle class. The evidence for this is that working-class people no longer look like early Gilbert O'Sullivan album covers.

The argument that the working class has ceased to be a significant force in society was first circulated by journalists writing for *Marxism Today* – though not by *Marxism Today* because it didn't have a circulation to speak of. It was, in any case, a curious name for a magazine written by ex-Marxists; it should have been called *Marxism Yesterday, Careerism Today*. Since it folded, its editor, Martin Jacques, has emerged as one of the leading authorities on the subject of what he thinks about the Labour Party. His view is that Labour cannot be elected until it has abandoned so many of its traditions that it is not so much a party as a few people round to dinner.

While I disagree with his view that the working class is a spent force, it *is* true that the trade union movement is no longer as effective as it was. These days, union leaders are so concerned not to alienate public opinion, that instead of calling *strikes*, they call *one-day* strikes. But it is impossible to have a class struggle on flexi-time. It's like trying to wage the Second World War on alternate Thursdays so as not to alienate

Switzerland. And the stated aim of union leaders in an industrial dispute is always to 'bring management to the table'. Well might one suggest an adjustment to the strategy: 'Bring them to their knees, fuck the table.' But perhaps I'm being very old-fashioned.

The leaders of the labour movement seem afraid to unleash the power of their members. When the poll tax rebellion was at its height and non-payers looked to the Labour Party for leadership, Neil Kinnock's advice amounted to, 'Don't break the law. Pay it now and get a receipt.'

There is also a crisis of ideology on the British Left. It is argued by some that Socialism is now irrelevant as an idea because of the changes in Eastern Europe. People who want to abuse left-wing paper sellers now find themselves saying, 'Why don't you go and live in er, er, . . . what are the Cubans up to?' But should those old Stalinist regimes be called socialist?[1] Stalin's doctrine in the twenties and thirties was what he called 'Socialism in One Country', but it seems doubtful that the country he was referring to was the Soviet Union. Moreover, he did not spread revolutionary ideas in Eastern Europe, he just asked Churchill if he could have it. Churchill's only condition was that, in return, Stalin should let him slaughter the Greek Communist Party and turn the country into a holiday resort. The question of the moment is, if the people of the former Iron Curtain countries can throw off the jackboot heel of authoritarianism, why can't the Cretans throw off the flip-flop of Club 18–30?

And why haven't we had a revolution in Britain? Britain is an increasingly divided and volatile society and yet somehow it remains stable. The idea that wealth and power are the birthright of the ruling class is increasingly questioned and yet they have

[1] No.

more wealth and power than ever. The reformist left is discredited but the revolutionary left is still small. Part of the answer lies with the effort that would be involved in the overthrow of the state. Most of us have a hard enough time organising a pub quiz team, let alone an insurrection.

So what conclusions can we draw about class in Britain in the late twentieth century? Is class analysis completely bogged down in definition, and what do we mean by 'definition'? Is it true that the old definitions are redundant and that we're all middle class now? And what implications will this have for sales of caviar and Pot Noodles? Is the new dynamic for change going to come from the growing underclass or will the traditional working-class movement rally and fight against the state? It's very easy to look back with the benefit of hindsight, so let's wait and do that.

Questions and Answers

There was always a vibrant question and answer session after this lecture. Here is a brief taste.

A student in Cambridge said, 'You pose as a man of the Left and yet you deride the only realistic forum for radical ideas, the Labour Party.'

I conceded, 'I vote Labour. To me, voting Labour is like wiping your bottom: I can't say I like doing it but you've got to – because you're in a worse mess if you don't.'

An irate woman in Aldershot Civic Hall aired this view, 'Mr Hardy, or should I call you Mr So-Called Hardy? You talk about class, but let me tell you; I was brought up among so-called working-class people and I don't need some wet-behind-the-ears left-wing pup telling me about the workers. They stop working any chance they get; tea breaks, dinner breaks, evenings, weekends. At my Ron's factory, half of them downed tools and went home the other day, just because they'd been made redundant or some such nonsense. Imagine if employers did that. You don't see the Queen Mum working to rule. I fought and died for this country. Morecambe and Wise never had to eff and blind to get a laugh. Call yourself a socialist – not too socialist to wear shoes, are you? There's no place like home, there's no place like home.'

I am still trying to think of an answer.

A man at Chandlers Ford Rotary Club issued this challenge: 'You say there is still a distinct working class. We all work, so what particular occupations do you consider to be working-class?'

I suggested as an example the nurses, to which he rejoindered, 'Well, I know a lot of nurses from middle-class backgrounds.'

I'm afraid my response was rather testy: 'Backgrounds? What have backgrounds got to do with it? When you're up to your elbows in kidneys and blood and shit and piss and pus, it's probably small consolation that you once rode in a gymkhana. I mean, if you're in hospital and you say, "Nurse I think I'm haemorrhaging", she doesn't say, "Well, I'd like to help you but I'm afraid I've just been reclassified into a different socio-economic bracket." Or sewage workers; how could you call sewage workers anything but working-class? If they were upwardly-mobile professionals they wouldn't go trudging through collapsing Victorian tunnels full of excrement and rats. They would hold consultancy periods and advise people on alternative methods of recycling their own excrement, and making tofu out of it.'

6. How To Be an Adult in Thought, Word and Deed

6 How To Be an Adult in Thought, Word and Deed

Being an adult is something that every grown-up is supposed to be able to do. But the wide age-range of the audiences for this lecture shows that there are many people whom our society defines as adults and yet who have absolutely no idea what they're doing. I wanted to help them in coming to terms with the responsibility of being mature individuals, and I confidently believe that I failed.

I have divided this lecture into three sections:
  1: how to conduct yourself;
  2: how to organise your personal finances; and
  3: how to do grown up things without going utterly to pieces and wanting your mum and dad to sort everything out for you.

How to Conduct Yourself

Firstly, how to conduct yourself. The fact of becoming an adult can come as quite a shock. I realised that it had started to happen to me when I was watching *Top of the Pops*, and I found myself thinking, 'Well, it all sounds the same, doesn't it? There's nothing you can tap your feet to. In the old days, we had the Sex Pistols and the Buzzcocks – something with a bit of a tune. Rap's not music – you can hear the words.'
  I also realised on my child's third birthday that being a father is not so much gaining a daughter as

becoming a parent. There are so many things I have
to do now. I have to provide. I have to plan for the
future. And I have to be able to drive without saying
'fuck'.

But even putting to one side the things I say to
and in front of my daughter, I'm constantly having
to think about what I'm saying because I'm having
to deal with different situations from the ones I was
dealing with ten years ago.[1] I can't walk into the bank
and say, 'Lend me ten quid till tomorrow, it'll save me
going to the bank.' I can't ring my solicitor back and
say, 'Sorry about that, I was just having a shit.' And I
can't tell a magistrate that the reason I haven't paid my
poll tax is that my little brother tore up my paying-in
book. I have to be one of those people I never thought
I'd be. I find myself saying things like, 'It is expensive
but not for what it is', and 'We're really only inviting
a few people so don't say anything to Patrick and Lor-
raine'.

But age is not the only factor affecting how we
conduct ourselves. There are a whole range of cultural, social and historical factors. For example, the
meaning of good manners varies around the world.
In some countries, belching at the dinner table is considered to be a great compliment to your host, and pro-
fuse vomiting is considered a great compliment to your
tour guide. And of course, within our culture, manners
are influenced by social class. An upper-class man
might dress for dinner; and I always try at least to
have my knickers on when the pizza man arrives.

Traditionally, different manners were also expected
of different sexes. Women are supposed to be more
dainty than men. You may well know the old maxim,
'Horses sweat, gentlemen perspire and ladies glow', or

---

[1]This is an ungainly sentence to read but if you say it out
loud it sounds all right.

the less well-known one, 'Ladies powder their noses, gentlemen use the bathroom and horses leave unbelievably huge turds all over the road'. And men are supposed to be gallant towards women. For example, if a man and a woman are walking along the pavement, the man should walk on the outside, so that the woman has to climb over the homeless.

Of course, many things which seem to be just pointless traditions today, often have practical reasons behind them. When houses were built overhanging the street, people would throw human waste out of their windows. So, if a lady walked on the inside, the gentleman would be hit instead of her. Mind you, I don't know what's more humiliating, being covered in excrement or being seen out on a date with someone who's covered in excrement.

According to custom, a man must woo. In the Middle Ages, a knight would win his lady's hand if she admired his jousting skills. So she'd end up married to someone who was no good in bed but couldn't half knock people off horses with a stick.

So, how we conduct ourselves is affected by history, nationality, sex, class and even occupation.

An Englishwoman might kiss me on the cheek and by that be saying, 'You are my friend.'

A Romanian man would kiss me on both cheeks and mean, 'Cheers then, be lucky.'

An Italian might kiss my hand and mean, 'Hello, you're the Pope.'

Someone in show business might kiss me on both cheeks and mean, 'Eat shit and die, whatever your name is.'

And a relative might kiss me on the forehead and say, 'He looks much better than he ever did when he was alive.'

The more adult we are, the less clear it is what people are saying to us. So you not only have to alter what you say, you must also interpret what is being said to you. If someone says, 'Tell me honestly', they mean 'Lie to me with conviction'.

Adult conversation is a long way from the kind of interaction we experience as children. Children might talk rubbish, but it's passionate, exuberant rubbish about games and food and telly and gravel-related injuries and how they nearly died when they were a baby. Children don't say, 'basically' or 'I kid you not'. They don't invoice you; they ask you for money for sweets, and if you say, 'How much do you want?' they don't say, 'Well, I wouldn't like to put a figure on it at the moment. I'll have to see how I get on and give you a bell later on this afternoon.' And if you won't give kids money for sweets, they don't send you a court summons; they just go around all the neighbours saying, 'Will you sponsor me?'

But being an adult is not necessarily to do with age. You can start or stop being an adult at any age. Child prodigies, for example, are terrifyingly grown-up. Of course, it is important to remember that they often have severe emotional problems, because it will cheer you up no end. The point is that these children seem in many ways to be very old, while old people can be just like children.

We think that second childhood is about incontinence and dementia, but it isn't necessarily. The old are like children because they fill up all the buses, talk too loud, eat sweets all day, watch any old rubbish they like on television, have filthy minds and refuse to remember anything you tell them. Of course, in other ways, they are not like children at all. Children have a lot more money for a start. And more energy.

It is a tragic fact that at the time in our lives when we have the most energy, there isn't really a lot we can do with it. Children use the same energy it would take to run the London Marathon in the average school playtime, doing things which are utterly pointless. And yet if I wanted to run the London Marathon, I would have to train for two years. To do something utterly pointless.

But it's not simply a matter of energy. There is behaviour which is perfectly acceptable for a child but not for an adult. Grown-ups join the Territorial Army and spend their whole weekends covered in mud, scrambling over assault courses, when all they really need is a water pistol and a climbing frame in the back garden. People become involved in complex webs of adultery and deceit, when a game of kiss chase would have got it out of their system. And how many people go through the mental and physical punishment of training to be a professional boxer, just for the skipping?

One situation when it is acceptable for supposed grown-ups to behave in a juvenile way is when they are in love. Then, you can snatch something from someone, run away from them along the beach and then fall down and tussle with them in the sand. In fact, if you're in a Hollywood movie, it's obligatory. But in general, conducting yourself as an adult means that there are lots of things you can no longer do, and lots of things you have to do which you didn't have to do before.

That is why adolescence, the supposed transition to adulthood, is a completely false start. True, your body starts to exhibit all the physical signs of maturity, apart from fat buttocks and baldness, but you don't really want to be an adult, because all the adults you know are so acutely aware of your adolescence that they've all gone peculiar. By the time you reach twenty, you've realised that adulthood is a thoroughly bad business, abandoned any pretensions to growing up and regressed completely. What you work out for yourself in those difficult years is that being an adult is not about freedom but *responsibility*.

But it is the burden of responsibility which eventually starts to turn you into somebody else, however much the Peter Pan in you rebels. These days, I find myself putting things in skips. Ten years ago I was taking them out. I found my first car in a skip. Ten years ago, it wasn't important to me that the car actually worked; it was only important that I could get the roof off, whether it was meant to come off or not. But, recently, I bought a proper car – a grown-up car. And my reason for doing this was 'To get me from A to B'. What a pitiful aspiration that is. Ten years ago, I didn't want to go to B; I wanted to go to exotic places like W.

Now, when I look through someone's window and see that they are having a party, I don't rush home, fill up an empty cider bottle, go back and say, 'Steve said it would be OK.'

And I'm not sure that I like the changes in myself. I comfort myself with the thought that 'I want different things at this point in my life'. The fact is, I want the same things. I just want them delivered.

Of course, many of my contemporaries are more grown-up or less grown-up than I am. I know a man of my age who, when he gets excited, hops like a little boy. His eyes get all big and round and fill with childlike wonder, and he says, 'Oh, brilliant!' Sadly, what makes him like that is garden furniture and the tax relief on endowment mortgages.

But I know other people who are completely irresponsible – people who are going to lay down some tracks in the studio when they've got their shit together; who come up with a scheme to fish old shopping trolleys out of the canal in order to do them up and sell them; and who, when required to fill in a landing card on an aeroplane, write, 'Terrorism' where it says 'Purpose of visit'.

By the by, a general note is that, when dealing with authority, a joke does not ease the tension. When you are asked, 'Have you worked in the last two weeks?' you will be taken at your word if you say, 'Yes, I've been ambassador to Turkey.'

If an official says to you, 'Could I see some means of identification?' it may hold things up if you retort, 'Do you want the appendix scar, or the mole on my arse?'

If you hear the question, 'Can you tell me what's in the boot of your car, miss?' and you reply, 'A bald tyre and a stash of ecstasy, I think, officer,' you may find that it's the wrong thing to say, because it turns out that what's actually in there is heroin, cocaine and a quantity of anything else they happen to have in stock.

When you are young and rebellious, you think everyone's out to get you. It is only when you've grown up that you realise they already have. That's why it's worthwhile knowing your rights. In Britain, we have no bill of rights or written constitution, so what rights do we have? Well, we can graze our geese on common land and take things back at Marks and Spencers.

As I get older, although I have not yet become a liberal myself, I have more and more respect for liberals. I am not talking about the Lib Dems necessarily, but proper old-fashioned liberals. When liberals hear about some abuse of power, they are outraged that such things can go on, determined that something must be done and moved to put pen to paper. Sometimes, they even put pen to placard. They turned out for the miners' demonstrations with their own personal, home-made banners each bearing an individual hand-written slogan, saying things like, 'Please, Mr Heseltine, think about what you are doing, and reconsider!' Which is a bugger of a chant to get behind.

The Left, on the other hand, are used to expecting the worst, and so are never surprised by anything the establishment does. This means that one can easily become jaded and apathetic. These days, my political activism is reduced to sitting in front of the television news saying 'bastards' periodically. I still turn up at the marches, but the main reason I go is that it enables me to get across London in half the time it takes by car.

Some people think that a part of growing up is the loss of idealism. But is there any physiological basis for the theory that we become more reactionary as we get older? It is true that our brain cells die off with age. We also tend to become nostalgic for the 'good old days'. I have to say, however, that the fact that I can remember good old days when there were school text books, full employment, a health service and streets where it was safe to walk somehow doesn't win me over to the cause of conservatism.

But, perhaps, however much we dislike the present system, we are less likely to want to revolt against it if we feel that we have a stake in it. You might be less inclined to throw up barricades in your street if it means donating your new dining-room table to the struggle. And we don't see Labour politicians on picket lines any more because they're worried about their suits getting creased.

But is the preservation of social order really in our long-term interest? Take this simple model. Let's say your principal assets are a car which you own and a video camera which you bought when they were the size of rocket-launchers and which you no longer use very often. On the liabilities side, you have a slight overdraft, an unpaid Access bill and a mortgage of sixty thousand pounds. Now, let's say civil unrest breaks out. Your car is turned over by rioters and your camcorder is smashed by police. But if the revolution succeeds, although you may have to put up the cast of *The Battleship Potemkin* in your spare room, you'll never have to pay off any of your debts.

Of course, there is always the danger that a right-wing backlash will exploit the power vacuum, enabling the building societies to take over, but what I hope to have demonstrated is that we often think we're doing much better out of the *status quo* than we actually are. Indeed, the more responsibilities we have, the more anger we might feel about things which didn't affect us as much before.

For example, I want my daughter to be able to read and write, but I don't want her to have to sit a three-hour paper every morning, invigilated by the managing director of a local building firm.

I want the police to protect my family from burglary and crack-dealing and murder, but I don't want them to protect me from black people who are driving.

And although I don't want to go to the cinema and see tasteless exploitative rubbish with entrails spilling out all over the place, if people want to eat Westler's hot dogs, that should be their choice.

So, how should you conduct yourself? Only you can decide. I shall now move on to the second part of this lecture, in which I tell you how to organise your personal finances.

How To Organise Your Personal Finances

As we've already seen, how we behave as an adult, and the kinds of things we say and do, are very much affected by our financial position. Someone who's just been turned out of their flat by a slum landlord and his thugs is unlikely to remark, 'Well, they do say moving house is one of the most stressful times in your life.'

But we can really only see things from our own perspective. I spent two years trying to move house[1] and

[1]See Chapter One.

now, when I see homeless people begging in the street, I catch myself thinking, 'Well at least you haven't got a full structural survey to pay for.' If you are in a state about something, it is of no comfort to be told that there is always someone worse off than you are, unless that person is someone you don't like. The fact that there are anonymous people all around the world who are having a much worse time than we are only succeeds in making us think, 'Well why don't they kill themselves?'

However, it is much easier to feel generous towards others when your own financial position is fairly secure.[1] So, how do you set about building a sound future for you and your family? Well, we all know that careful savings and investment are important, but do you really want to be one of those people who listen to *Money Box*? Do you want to be an avaricious, petit-bourgeois inadequate who knows whether a child is more tax-efficient than a loft conversion? Do you want to have one Telecom share and a tidy little sum tucked away in an Instant Savings Super Gold Portfolio Account whereby they give you a shiny folder for your statements with a picture of old people laughing on the cover. And you can decide whether the bank gives you the interest annually or just keeps it?

Of course, you don't have to have a lot of money to become a saver. You can open a building society account with as little as one pound. But what's the point? If you've only got one pound, I should have thought you're likely to need to get at your money rather quickly. You're not going to want to put it in the Abbey National and have to take the bus to the High Street any time you want to dip into it. Everyone is supposed to be making provision for their futures, when most people don't even know if

[1]This fact does make one wonder why the rich are such stingy bastards.

they can get through the present without robbing a security van. Every time I walk past the bank and a man with a blue helmet walks out carrying a sack, I think, 'I bet if I just grabbed the money and ran, he'd be so surprised he wouldn't even bother to run after me.'

You're probably thinking that I am not the best qualified person to be giving financial advice. But who is? Ten years ago, property was a sound investment, the Docklands Development had a great future, and the Bank of Credit and Commerce International was the friend of small business people. Now it seems that the only wise investors are the people who never threw their flares away.

How can I give financial advice when financial advisers have been so roundly discredited? In the nineteen-eighties, so many of us were stung by young charlatans with the answers to all our money questions. Those of us who get tearful and sweaty at the thought of anything more complicated than a cashpoint card, thought, 'Praise God. At last there are people whose job it is purely to help me organise my life, with no taint of an interest of their own, who are entirely independent and slaves to no man's commission. Tell me, tell me, oh wise one, what's a mortgage?'

At the time when I consulted an Independent Financial Adviser about getting a mortgage, by sheer luck, the whole interview was recorded by someone from *Which?* magazine who was doing a survey of loud waistcoats. Here is our exchange in full. Let it be a warning to you all.

    IFA   Come in, come in, sit down. Jeremy, isn't it?
    JH   Yes.
    IFA   Now, Jeremy – can I call you Mr Hardy?
    JH   By all means.
    IFA   Now, Mr Hardy, you want to buy a flat,

	and you want to borrow the money.
JH	Yes.
IFA	And I expect you'd like a bit of tax relief.
JH	What's that?
IFA	Money.
JH	Oh, yes, please.
IFA	OK. Now, do you think you'd like a little bit or a lot?
JH	A lot?
IFA	Businessman, I can tell. Nothing wrong with that. OK, so, have a look at this bar chart. You've got two bars there. Which one would you say is a lot?
JH	That one.
IFA	The biggest one?
JH	Yes.
IFA	Well, you've just pointed to the flexible-rate insurance mortgage with the National Loan Sharks Corporation.
JH	Did I?
IFA	Yessiree. Now let me talk you through the NLSC package. We're after tax relief, right? And the more the loan costs, the more tax relief you'll get.
JH	So I want the most expensive mortgage available?
IFA	Can't hold you back, can I? Now, there is a risk with this mortgage. Life's a risk. You take a gamble when you put a grand on the gees-gees, don't you? So that's what National Loan Sharks do: put your money on the horses. Now, do you know about insurance mortgages?
JH	No.
IFA	Right, well, you're gonna die. Fact. We don't like it but it's tough titty. So, how do you feel about leaving the wife and kids in

	the shit so your missus has to go on the game and the kids die of rickets?
JH	Well . . .
IFA	Got any kids yet?
JH	Not yet.
IFA	Firing blanks?
JH	No! We'll have lots of kids, probably. I don't know. I –
IFA	So, in other words, you want insurance. Now, with an ordinary mortgage, if you pop your clogs from, let's say, cancer . . . Let's say you've got a malignant tumour now.
JH	Have I?
IFA	Yeah, you're riddled, falling to bits. So, you're dying in other words. We're all dying but especially you. Now, a normal mortgage is paid off when you die. But supposing you live; you have to pay it off yourself. So you die at what, thirty-six because you've got a tumour, and you've got to pay interest on the loan right up until you die. Now, with an insurance mortgage, you die younger but better looking, but you don't want to lose your tax relief, so the Waiver Premium Unlimited Gullibility Clause allows your family to keep paying the mortgage until the endowment matures when you would have been ninety, and the lump sum pays off all the interest you would have paid if you'd been alive, leaving your mortgage untouched, so the kids have still got a nice big loan to pay off in their retirement. Sounds pretty tempting, doesn't it?
JH	Well, I'm in your hands. Where do I sign?

That rather salutary conversation brings me to the subject of tax. The whole tax system is perverse. For example, the Inland Revenue tell us that we should find out whether we are entitled to a rebate. In other words, they have taken money which they should not have taken, but might give it back if we beg them. And if you get this money back, you are supposed to be over-joyed. That's like having your wallet stolen and then being cock-a-hoop when your Blockbuster Video card turns up in a litter bin. Well, it's a bit like that. And I wouldn't mind paying tax if the government spent it on good stuff, but paying tax under the Tories is like giving a Waterford crystal vase to an eight-week-old baby.

VAT I cannot fathom. I know it's designed to screw the poor, that bit I've got the hang of. But I am self-employed. I have to charge people VAT. And I'm not mature enough to do that. If I do some work, I'm supposed to charge VAT and then give the money to Her Majesty's Customs and Excise, who give it back to the people I charged it from. And the money actually has to change hands. It wouldn't be so bad if you could do it with matchsticks or chocolate buttons. At least then you could turn it into a game. But this stuff's for real. You don't mess with these people. If you forget to write something down, they don't say, 'Oh don't worry about it, just buy us a drink next time you see us.' You're under investigation. They want to rip up your floorboards to search for Spanish doubloons. Go through your laundry and sniff all your pants. Why won't everyone just leave me alone?

This brings me to the third and final part of this lecture: How to do grown-up stuff without going utterly to pieces and wanting your mum and dad to sort everything out for you.

But I have already shown that I can't cope with

life. So there's not much point in me going on with this and I'd like to stop now, if that's all right.

Questions and Answers

There was always an uneasy silence at the end of this lecture, and there was a reluctance on the part of audiences to come forward with any questions. In fact, I never did get any questions apart from these three:

A woman at the Lowestoft Festival of the Human Voice, told me, 'It is wonderful to hear a live speaker. We have brought all of our nine children. They simply love recitals and readings and hearing local craftspeople talking about ceramics. They really don't miss the television. We got rid of the blessed thing when we moved up from London a year ago, although we let the kids go to neighbours if they want to watch *Horizon* or anything to do with the environment. Don't you think children are much better off without the goggle-box always being there?'
I thought for a moment and said, 'Oh, fuck off and leave me alone.'

A teenage boy at a Preston Comprehensive asked, 'Don't you think life is what you make it?'
I told him, 'No, life is what you're left with when nothing else comes off.'

The third question came from an elderly man at Droitwich Assembly Hall. If anyone was capable of talking about getting older, then this venerable old gent certainly was. He asked me, 'Could you make a move, sonny? They've all gone home now and I'm locking up in a couple of minutes.'

Afterword

It is said that a man does not choose to be a public speaker: he is chosen. But it is not said very often, or by anyone other than me. You might say that I have a gift, and that no man can choose his gift, unless he has a voucher. I hesitate to call it genius, because, to use the wise words of Thomas Edison, 'Genius is one per cent of all inspiration; and perspiration is nine tenths of the law.' Let's just say that eloquence is a skill which some are lucky enough to have or you don't.

But, whatever it was that guided me to become a communicator of ideas, I hope you have enjoyed the chance to read at first hand what can at best be a second-hand experience. When the spoken word appears on paper it is inevitable that something is los . A reader, as opposed to a listener, can never feel the impact of the conviction, the passion or the saliva of a platform speaker. On the other hand, the reader has a chance to savour morsels which might pass straight through an open-mouthed audience before they can digest them. But enough of this shit.

I hope that you will want to read these lectures again and again and again and again.

Some of you will not have read them at all, and have just flicked through to the end of the book to find out what happens.

Some of you are not old enough to read and are being read to by parents or guardians because they hope that even the tiniest can share in the knowledge which these tracts impart, or because you won't go to sleep.

This is a book to be enjoyed by anyone, anywhere, at any time of the year. Whoever and wherever you are, I wish you all a very happy Christmas.